IN THE GRAVEST EXTREME:

The Role of the Firearm in Personal Protection

by

Massad F. Ayoob

Available from   *Police Bookshelf*
                  P.O. Box 122
                  Concord, NH 03301 USA

Nineteenth Printing

ISBN 0-936297-00-1

*To my mother, Mary Elizabeth Ayoob,
who approved when my father taught me
defensive weaponry at an early age . . .
and thus probably preserved me to write
this book.*

Massad F. Ayoob

About the Author

Massad F. Ayoob grew up with weapons. The only son of a jeweler who had been maimed for life by an armed criminal—and who had killed that man and crippled his accomplice forever with expertly-returned gunfire—he came early to the subtle art and science of weaponcraft, learning gun safety and marksmanship beginning at the age of four. He won his first of hundreds of pistol awards as a teenager, and was captain of a first string pistol team at 22. He got his first .22 pistol at age 11, his first .45 automatic for his twelfth Christmas. Working in the family jewelry store part time, he began carrying a concealed and loaded .38 before he reached puberty.

Today, Ayoob is recognized internationally as one of the world's leading authorities on police weaponry. A sworn officer with a municipal New England department 1972-1980, he was a certified weapons instructor with the Advanced Police Training Program of New Hampshire (teaching weapons and chemical agents to full time police officers, with a rank of associate professor of police science), and is guest instructor at the Smith & Wesson Academy and the New Hampshire Institute of Self Defense (Uechi-ryu karate).

Ayoob is handgun editor of GUNS magazine, field editor of AMERICAN HANDGUNNER, associate editor of LAW ENFORCE-MENT HANDGUN DIGEST, contributing editor of LAW AND ORDER, and feature editor of the police professional journals TROOPER and PATROLMAN. He is the author of "Fundamentals of Modern Police Impact Weapons," considered the definitive police manual on the use of striking tools such as nightsticks. His name is familiar to many police officers, who are taught to shoot with the "Ayoob Wedge Hold" or who carry their nightsticks in "Ayoobstyle baton rings."

A champion pistol shot, Ayoob has been a member of several All-State and State Champion handgun teams in both bullseye and combat. In 1978, he ranked 6th in the United States in tournament pistol match winnings. He holds the record for winnings at the Second Chance "Street Combat National Championship" event, placed first master at the Fraternal Order of Police national combat shoot, and holds two unofficial records for hunting big game with a handgun.

Before becoming a policeman, and since, Ayoob was involved in several life-threatening situations wherein he had to draw a gun, and in which his armed control of the scene probably saved the lives of himself and others. He experienced more lethal threat situations in his police capacity.

This led him to realize that the average citizen who keeps guns for self defense has little real grasp of what the laws are that govern such instruments—the laws of the land as well as the laws of survival. It is for this reason that he wrote "In the Gravest Extreme: the Role of the Firearm in Civilian Self-Defense."

More than a year before publication, chapter excerpts appeared in GUNS magazine. They were met with acclaim from judges and lawyers, cops and armed citizens. "Never before," many said, "has anyone told the truth about what happens to you if you use a gun for defense." A few hard-core gun nuts wrote to say that Ayoob was "telling us we can't kill bad guys." A publisher of gun books that had wanted to print the book backed out, saying, "You're telling a lot of gun owners things they don't want to hear." Others accused Ayoob of writing "A guide on how to kill criminals and get away with it." All were, in a sense, correct in their assessments.

Every other book on self-defense with firearms has begun with the draw and ended with the last shot. Ayoob sought to teach the armed public what would happen to them afterward, and what they had to think about before. This is the core of "In the Gravest Extreme."

Thus, this text does not delve deeply into how to make a quick draw or handload super-destructive ammunition. Ayoob is an authority on these subjects, and his articles published in police and technical firearms journals on these subjects would add up to several books. Ayoob merely capsulized his recommendations of guns, ammo, holsters, and firing positions to what works best for the untrained beginner to journeyman classes of gun carrier. Those seeking more sophisticated information on armed defense should read his book "Gunfighting for Police: Advanced Tactics and Techniques," soon to be offered by Charles C. Thomas of Springfield, Ill., the world's leading publisher of police training manuals.

The principles put forth in the book you hold in your hands are based on law, and the mood of the American courts. Ayoob doesn't agree with all of them. But he feels that anyone who chooses to arm himself against criminals should know these things.

Ayoob works in the criminal justice system, with experience as a street cop, prosecuting officer, and certified expert witness for both the prosecution and the defense in cases involving weapons and armed citizens. He knows what he is talking about . . . and anyone who owns a gun and has thought about using it in self defense, needs to know what Ayoob is talking about, too.

Massad Ayoob is a champion combat pistol shooter and a recognized expert on law enforcement, and also an award winning writer who researched the question of armed defense to the ultimate possible degree. He didn't include state laws or case precedents, which are too quickly and frequently overturned, instead telling the reader to get a handle on his own state laws and court moods through study of the prevailing statutes, review of precedents in his state, and consultation with his own attorney.

Ayoob, who has faced deadly danger as a civilian and as a cop, and survived because he had a gun he knew how and when to use, has written the ultimate guide to the ultimate level of self defense—killing force directed against those who would kill wantonly, summary yet legal capital punishment for savage criminals who place law abiding citizens in the gravest extreme of mortal danger.

Table of Contents

                                                                      Page
Chapter 1 - Introduction   1
Chapter 2 - Self-Defense and Lethal Force   5
Chapter 3 - The Dangerous Myth of Citizen's Arrest 27
Chapter 4 - Samaritans with Guns 33
Chapter 5 - Women and Guns 35
Chapter 6 - A Gun in Your Store 43
Chapter 7 - A Gun in Your Home 51
Chapter 8 - A Gun in Street........................... 65
Chapter 9 - A Gun in Your Car 69
Chapter 10 - Deterrent Effect of Defense Handguns 75
Chapter 11 - Common Sense About Carrying Guns 81
Chapter 12 - High Price of Handgun Machismo 89
Chapter 13 - Choosing a Defense Gun 95
Chapter 14 - What Caliber for Self Defense................ 103
Chapter 15 - Basic Gunfighting Techniques................ 111
Chapter 16 - Gun Safety 121
Chapter 17 - The Aftermath 127

Chapter 1
Introduction

When I decided to write this book, I resolved not to fill it with grisly cases of criminals shot by citizens in self-defense. Those who believe that the private citizen should not be permitted to possess defensive firearms rely heavily on anecdotes of murder for shock effect; Carl Bakal's "No Right to Bear Arms" is a case in point. Actually, almost every incident Bakal and the others depict can be argued either way. Their opinion is that each atrocity could have been averted if the assailants could have been prevented from having guns; my contention is that almost every one could have been prevented or mitigated had the intended victims been armed and able to fight back against their murderers. An exception is the accidental shooting, a statistically unlikely occurence that can, in my opinion, be eliminated by proper training.

This book makes no attempt to convince the private citizen to acquire or carry firearms. It speaks to those who have already made the decision to do so, and endeavors only to advise them in the legal, ethical, and practical use of the deadly weapons they already own.

Perhaps it should be clarified at this point that the author believes personally that the citizen has the right to kill in defense of innocent life; the dead attacker waived his own right to live when he threatened to wrongfully deprive a victim of his. It is questionable whether anyone has the moral right, although the legal right still exists in many places, to use deadly force solely in defense of property. A housebreaker should be shot only if he presents a deadly danger to the innocent people therein, not to prevent his making off with the family silver. At the same time, one can understand the reasoning of a shopkeeper who kills a robber to prevent his escaping with stolen money, if the increasing depredations of such criminals have made it impossible for the merchant to get insurance, and the stolen receipts literally represent food out of his family's mouths.

Still, some states forbid anyone to kill over their money or anyone else's; so long as such laws are accompanied by a system that guarantees reparations for losses to criminals they should be universal and will eventually become so.

This book was written to correct the dangerous misconceptions on the part of many as to when they can exert the deadly force of the guns they have decided in advance that they may use for self-protection. Too many people believe they can shoot suspected criminals when, in fact, they may have no right to do so. Too many people are incapable of using their guns in a combat situation with sufficient expertise to either prevent an armed criminal from taking innocent lives, or to be sure of not hitting bystanders with their own stray bullets. Both knowledge and ability should be pre-requisites for the privilege of carrying a gun in public. It is my personal opinion that every applicant for a carry permit should pass a written examination on self-defense and lethal force laws, and a close-range qualification run over a combat pistol shooting course.

Some gun owners may consider this a suggested abrogation of their Constitutional rights. On the contrary, it is the failure to institute such controls that may eventually terminate the privilege of carrying concealed weapons for personal safety. Every well-intentioned citizen who shoots a shoplifter or petty thief—or a bystander, with a wild bullet—causes a public clamor to take away the privilege of keeping guns for personal defense, not only from him, but from me and from every other responsible citizen who chooses to arm himself.

It is a privilege that cannot be denied to the public by those who refuse to exercise or understand it themselves. The rate of crime against the person has increased at a rate that far outpaces the numerical and technical growth of the crime prevention community. The police establishment does not pretend that it can protect every citizen from every fatal or crippling assault. Indeed, there are many state and local governments whose ability to protect their constituents has actually declined. For the past few years, for instance, lack of funds has prohibited New York City from hiring new policemen, and attrition of resignations and what not has reduced the ranks of New York's finest from 35,000 to approximately 24,000 men. Yet the administrators of that city advocate reducing the privileges of private firearms ownership. The government that cannot protect the public must not strip them of the right to protect themselves.

And, in truth, the firearm is the only really effective means of defense against vicious, homicidal assault. Not for nothing are guns called equalizers. Nothing else can serve this function for the individual, law-abiding citizen. Clubs, knives, unequal physical strength, a gang's force of numbers—these are the equalizers to which the criminal resorts. They are, by their nature, weapons to which the average man or woman has no recourse, unless he or she either possesses brute strength, or travels in a pack.

It will be said by some that this book teaches the reader to kill criminals and get away with it. I prefer to think that it teaches him to stay alive in certain desperate situations; the emphasis is not so much on the taking of life as the relieving of threat to life. Far from encouraging the reader to take life, it advises great practical and moral restraint in the use of the lethal power the reader already possesses. I believe that the taking of one citizen's life by another is an unnatural act, justified only as a last desperate escape from grave criminal danger. I think this philosophy will be evident in the following chapters.

Nor do I believe that this book will be of use to anyone but law-abiding citizens interested only in self-defense. The practical techniques are not assault-oriented, and in any case, if criminals read to improve their professional skills, they would long ago have absorbed the police procedural textbooks and become even harder to apprehend than they already are.

This book is one answer to our society's collective fear of individual attack. Some may be shocked that a book could be published teaching ordinary people how to use deadly force, for any purpose. Perhaps, in the last analysis, the only really shocking thing is that such a book needed to be written.

Chapter 2
Self-Defense and
Lethal Force

There is a remarkable degree of confusion among the general public as to just when lethal force is warranted. Other important concepts of degree of force in defense situations not only aren't fully understood, but are often completely unknown to some who legally go armed. Let us consider, first, the nature and use of deadly force.

Lethal Force

Depending on circumstances, almost any form of physical assault is potentially deadly force: any form or intensity of attack that can be expected to jeopardize or terminate the life of he who is attacked. A blow of the hand delivered powerfully and deliberately to a vital part of the body may be construed as deadly force, so long as it can be shown that it was struck with the intention, or predictable likelihood, of killing. The court is more likely to interpret it as such if he who delivers the blow is (a) physically much stronger than the victim, (b) a professional fighter or, in some cases, a proven expert in the martial arts, or (c) an assailant who attacks with extreme savagery, perhaps gratuitously raining blows and kicks upon his opponent, even after the latter has fallen or otherwise given up the conflict.

In the great majority of cases, however, deadly force means the use of a lethal weapon, be it a knife or gun, or a makeshift bludgeon, stabbing instrument, or garrotte. We are concerned here primarily with the use of firearms. The "deadly force" definitions of certain unarmed physical assaults, are relevant to law-abiding citizens who do not carry weapons but may become involved in a mortal combat; still the principal interest of unarmed lethal force is as it relates to provoking the *armed* response of a law-abiding citizen. We therefore move into . . .

Disparity of Force

This is among the vaguest concepts in self-defense law. It is tied inextricably with legal doctrines of "equal force". Essentially, it is the analysis of "equal force" in determining whether the given unarmed assault situation calls for armed counter-attack.

The "equal force" doctrines require the law-abiding citizen to respond to attack with little or no more force than that which he perceives is being directed against him. However, the law recognizes that great degrees of difference may exist between the potential physical force of the victim, and that commanded or levied by his attacker(s).

This disparity of force between the unarmed combatants is measured in one of two ways: it exists if the victim is attacked by one who is physically much stronger or younger than he, or by two or more attackers of equal or similar size. Disparity of force is an *interpretive* concept; few if any states have recognized court precedents in this area. If the question comes up, it is usually considered in the catch-all area of the "reasonableness" of the defender's response, which we'll discuss later.

Therefore, it is difficult to break the disparity concept down into hard and fast terms. There are no height, weight, and age charts to indicate the exact point where unarmed, equal force becomes disparate. Obviously a 5-foot-6, 130-pound man of sixty is not on equal footing with a 250-pound, nineteen-year-old assailant. But what if the defender is a strapping, athletic, fiftyish man, and the attacker is a physically puny youth? Where the physical advantages are mixed, the court will either consider the opponents equally matched, or determine relative command of force from other inputs—the savagery of the attack, for instance, or the circumstances leading up to it.

With regard to multiple opponents, we again have different complexions. Obviously, a man who uses a gun on three unarmed twelve-year olds is going to be crucified in court, no matter how much damage they might have inflicted. Another situation, one more likely to crop up, is an assault by two or three muggers. No one will question your actions if you use a gun in this case, but where do you stand after your gun has reduced their number to a single, unarmed attacker?

There is no set answer; a definitive court ruling is hard to find since the vast majority of self-defense shootings have involved *mano-a-mano* confrontations. From a practical standpoint, of course, the use of the gun on the remaining assailant seems indicated if he continues the fray. Unarmed attack is by definition a face-to-face encounter; if he stays in the fight, he is probably close enough to wrest the weapon from you and kill you with it. If he runs, of course, you cannot shoot. The fact that he has joined in a group attack, which can constitute deadly force, and is continuing the assault, would seem a reasonable indication that he intends to inflict great harm upon you; the fact that you know him only as a member of a gang of muggers indicates to you that he is a violent individual, and capable of carrying out the violent intent obviously implied in his actions. One factor that can change this is the degree of the last assailant's response. If he stands back, neither fleeing nor attacking, but stunned into immobility at the sight of his comrades being shot down, he is not offering at that moment the kind of direct threat that calls for a killing response. His closeness to you and his demeanor will be the determinants of your reaction.

When attacked by two or more people, the defender generally has had the right to shoot any member of the gang who obviously shares the group's criminal intent,[1] even though he may be hanging back slightly while those in the forefront of the group deliver most or all of the actual blows. It is questionable, however, that this rule can be counted upon; a contemporary court might very well rule that only those making the actual assault could be subjected to homicidal defensive force, over-ruling precedents to the contrary. In any case, the imperatives of the moment will indicate that you use the gun on the closest, most dangerous members of the gang *anyway*; those who who are on the outside edge of the group present you with a much lesser danger, and unless you hit one with a wild shot, it is unlikely that you will have to go with this rather uncertain legal defense. It's probably just as well.

All this, of course, relates to situations involving actual attack, or the clear and imminent threat of same. That recurring nightmare of being pushed around and terrorized by a bunch of

---

[1]Warren on Homicide, vol. 1, p. 642 "Where several are apparently preparing to join in an attack on defendant, his right of self-defense extends to each participant."

wise-ass punks or delinquents, may not call for the use of deadly force.

An obscene insult to one's wife or child; a glob of spit on one's shoes or a cigarette butt flicked into the face; a snotty challenge of "What the fuck you gonna do about it, fuckface?" thrown by a group of punks standing three or four abreast, a few feet away from you, blocking the sidewalk—all these and similar provocations can trigger the blackest, deadliest rage in a typical man, especially if they occur in front of his family.

Yet an armed response is not necessarily warranted at this point. Only words and gestures have passed, and these are not sufficient to create a killing situation in the eyes of the law. Even if they mockingly strike you, you may not be justified in using your gun: one Illinois court found that a slap from a naked hand, delivered without intent to commit great bodily harm, was not sufficient to make the killing of the slapper justifiable.

What will determine your degree of legal response will be a mixture of actions on your part and theirs. Some states require you to attempt to withdraw; others give you the right to stand your ground in any place where you are entitled to be. Irrespective of your local laws, it is a good idea to retreat or beg off anyway: from a practical standpoint, you are at a disadvantage. Your multiple opponents are probably close enough to disarm you if they're fast enough; if your family is present, they are close enough to be grabbed as hostages, or hit by a stray bullet if a gunfight breaks out or if someone grapples with you for your sidearm.

From the moral standpoint, it may really be that the opponents intend only to show off at your expense. This is, admittedly, hard to accept when you are the one being terrorized. Also, it may be reasonable to assume that their wanton troublemaking may precede a more serious expression of terrorism.

The principal moral consideration is the effect that a shooting incident might have on those family members present. Violent death by gunfire is a gruesome, traumatizing thing to watch, especially if it is committed by a parent before the eyes of a child close enough to the unfolding situation to realize, now or later, if the act may not have been entirely justified. Too many American men think that an act of violence will create or reinforce the respect of those they love. The belief is a by-product of that part of the American spirit that lives vicariously through entertainment media which glorify physical violence. Perhaps too often, this belief is well founded, but an act of extreme violence in front of your loved ones can still be a deep emotional shock that can alter forever, and in a most unpleasant way, the light in which they look at you. If only for this reason, be *really* sure of the danger before you decide to employ a deadly weapon against multiple antagonists whose motives are uncertain.

Equal Force

Nowhere can a man legally respond to an assault of slight degree with deadly force. In a few places, the law clearly specifies that equal force must be exactly that: the attacked can respond with no more force than that by which he is threatened—slap for slap, kick for kick, weapon for deadly weapon.

A more practical approach would be to respond to each level of the assault with a degree of force sufficiently, but not greatly, superior to that with which one is threatened. There are two advantages to a *slightly* greater degree of force: obviously, it places the defender in a more secure tactical position, but perhaps more important, it can discourage the assailant from continuing his attack to the point where a shooting becomes necessary.

A *vastly* greater degree of force—drawing a weapon that threatens deadly force before the same has been threatened against he who draws—voids the claim of reasonable self-defense if a killing occurs.

Equal force is another concept that is open for interpretation; like disparity of force, it will probably be relegated to a consideration in determining "reasonableness" in an actual court situation.

Reasonableness

Almost without exception, "reasonable force" is the concept upon which the court disposition of a self-defense shooting will ultimately rest. "The judgment of a reasonable man" is a standard that pervades the American system of justice. Some call it a vague yardstick, others a flexible one; it is certainly the most practical determinant, given the great variety of circumstances under which it becomes the arbiter of legal judgment.

It gives the court an avenue whereby extenuating considerations may be pursued beyond the letter of laws conceived by men who had never anticipated certain situations. It permits each case to be judged on its own particular circumstances, rather than being pigeon-holed into one category or another of self-defense law.

When Can You Pull the Trigger?

American laws universally condone homicide ONLY WHEN UNDERTAKEN TO ESCAPE IMMINENT AND UNAVOIDABLE DANGER OF DEATH OR GRAVE BODILY HARM. A great many states allow the use of lethal force in protection of property, though the majority stipulate that this privilege exists only during home robberies involving breaking and entering. Even this is not sufficient in some states, which require you to first be in deadly jeopardy before you pull the trigger, even in your own home.

Various statutes permit the citizen to shoot an offender caught in the course of any felony from burglary to, in at least one case, sodomy. Perhaps the most striking thing one notices in comparing the codes of the various states is how often homicide is justified by the civilian "when committed in attempting, by lawful ways and means, to apprehend any person for any felony committed, or in lawfully suppressing any riot, or in keeping and preserving the peace."

Such codes are terrifyingly broad. To many minds, they conjure images of rednecked vigilantes swarming the streets with shotguns to "Keep and preserve the peace."

These rules are not general knowledge even in the states where they apply, since there have been few test cases.

It is fortunate that so few people are aware that these statutes exist—fortunate not only for the potential victims, but for the law-abiding citizen who believes everything he reads.

The key phrases in these deceptive statutes are "lawful ways and means." The casual layman reading such a statute could interpret it to mean that he is justified in using deadly force to stop any felony or any fleeing felon, when in fact, such action does *not* constitute lawful means or ways.

Although many states lump all justifiable homicides together, it is proper to have separate definitions for police and civilians; even when such separation does not exist it is generally assumed

10

that police authority to use deadly force in apprehension of felons exceeds the authority of civilians. The general precept that cops may shoot to stop escaping crooks is coming under increasingly heavy attack, and statutory evolution is already beginning to narrow this authority.

There are many circumstances under which shooting an escaping criminal may *not* be justified, unless the felon represents a clear and present danger to the general public so long as he is at large. For instance, a police officer who kills a fleeing car thief may be disciplined or indicted, unless it is shown that the stolen car was being driven so recklessly as to make a collision involving innocents likely enough that the officer had to terminate the pursuit by gunfire, to end the threat to innocent motorists and pedestrians.[2]

Once, in the course of conducting a firearms training program for a 19-man police department, the author found that most of the officers believed they were authorized to kill a fleeing criminal, in a car or on foot, if that was the only manner of capture open to them. Several of the patrolmen cited a state code which allowed the peace officer to kill a known felon if he could stop him in no other way. In another community a few miles away, great public furor had arisen over a local cop who had shot a running unarmed fugitive in the back of the head, moments after he had swung at the officer.

I contacted the chief of the criminal division of that state's Attorney General's Office for a definitive ruling one way or the other. I wanted an authority that either I could quote in the negative when I told them not to shoot to capture, or *they* could quote in the positive if they ever did.

"Yes," I was told, "They have the statutory right to use lethal force to effect capture. But that's not to say they won't get into a shitload of trouble if they do." Statutory authority does not always give the definite power it implies. The case of the patrolman in the other town proved that.

Even for cops, there are many subtle considerations involved in shooting-to-capture, considerations which seldom if ever appear in the statutes or criminal codes concerning justifiable homicide. Has the suspect committed the felony before the eyes of the of-

---

[2]"Vehicular Aspects of Police Gunfight Situations," by Massad F. Ayoob, LAW & ORDER Magazine, Oct., 1972.

in the statutes or criminal codes concerning justifiable homicide. Has the suspect committed the felony before the eyes of the officer who pulls the trigger, or has he otherwise been positively identified as the felon? If he has been identified, does any reason therefore exist why he can't be picked up later? Is he armed, and/or so violent that his freedom constitutes a real threat to the community?

All these and more must stay the policeman's trigger finger, much less the civilian's.

A major legal consideration will further prevent the private citizen from shooting: *once the threat of assault has passed, and the felon is no longer jeopardizing him, the civilian's shooting of the felon will no longer be considered self-defense.*

We now come back to the greater rule of justifiable homicide in general—"only to escape imminent and unavoidable death or grave bodily harm." This, not the policeman's rules, is the standard of judgment that will be applied to you, the private citizen.

Another important self-defense concept that is relevant here is that the privilege of using lethal force to stop a felony, if that privilege exists at all, *ends after the fact of the felony.* If you can shoot at all, you can shoot only to prevent or terminate the commission of the crime itself; to shoot the criminal after the crime has been committed, no matter how long or short the time interval, is either to avenge or to punish the crime. No individual has the right to do either.

Even if you do have the legal right to shoot in defense of your property alone, and consider the act moral, the law is generally clear that you can do so only between the time the offender actually shows his intention, and the time he leaves off, whether he has been successful or not.

The moment at which the opponent turns away, and the moment he curtails his assault, are not necessarily the same. He may be running only for better cover, or for a better weapon.

If he has given up the combat in earnest, don't pursue him (forget that vaguely worded law in your state that may seem to allow you to use deadly force in capturing a felon). Many states permit you to "pursue until he is no longer a danger to the defendant," in other words, to chase him away.

But there is still another tricky legal doctrine waiting to trap you if you chase a thief or erstwhile opponent. Your quarry could not claim self-defense if he had hurt you in the initial struggle, since he was in the wrong and self-defense is a privilege reserved for the innocent. But after he made an obvious attempt to desist and escape, that conflict ended. Now, as you pursue him, remember that when you catch up you will not necessarily be continuing the initial confrontation, but in the eyes of the law, opening a new one—*opening a confrontation in which the criminal will be blameless since you, not he, are now the aggressor.* He is trying to avoid the combat, and you are now carrying the fight to him (remember, a past incident is not grounds for deadly force in the immediate present, no matter how recently it occurred). Therefore, he now possesses the privilege of self-defense.

He can now, in short, turn around and kill you, and get away with it.

Your own position at this point is debatable. The court may feel you are still entitled to wear the legally-protective mantle of self-defense, especially if you can cite a state code authorizing you to use force to effect the capture of a felon. Others may decide that when you took up pursuit of a man who had retired from the fray, you were no longer defending yourself, since there was no longer anything to defend yourself against. You, on the other hand, chased a non-belligerent and threatened to use deadly force on him, or *did* use such force, when in fact you had no legal right to do so. You have violated a fistful of self-defense codes: the man was not putting you in danger of being killed or crippled when you pulled the gun on him after the chase (if you *were* in such danger, that's another thing, and you're probably in the clear. But now we're talking about criminals who are just trying to get away without violence). Your motive might be construed as a malicious or misguided intent to perform an unauthorized execution.

For these reasons alone, pursuit should almost never be undertaken. The great practical danger it presents to both you and any bystanders, will be considered elsewhere as a gunfighting problem.

ALTOGETHER, THE BEST RULE IS TO RESORT TO DEADLY FORCE ONLY WHEN LIFE AND LIMB ARE IN JEOPARDY.

Retreat, Withdrawal, and Avoidance

Our model guideline refers to imminent and *unavoidable* danger of death or grave bodily harm. The great majority of states require that you *avoid* the conflict, and its potentially homicidal outcome. It is best to *withdraw*, leaving the scene entirely. At the very least, the citizen is expected to *retreat* from the belligerent party who threatens him. How far need he retreat? Until he can retreat no farther, say most rulings; it could be called a "back-to-the-wall law." Other states, perhaps more realistically, eliminate the requirement of retreat if the onslaught is so savage there is no time to escape, or if turning one's back or leaving cover to escape would increase the victim's vulnerablity. A few states have eliminated entirely the need to give way, and permit the attacked party to stand his ground, so long as he has the right to be where he is.

One circumstance under which no one need give ground is an assault within the confines of the home. That "a man's home is his castle" is not merely a catch phrase, but a by-word of the legal system. The dwelling is considered an extension of the man, a part of his body-proper. Indeed, at least one state, New Mexico, takes this concept so seriously that one damaging the home may be subject to the lethal force of the owner if that is what it takes to make him desist. Actually, the New Mexico statute is not as radical as it seems at first glance: while it conjures in the layman's mind an image of a person being blown away for throwing rocks against the aluminum siding, a more serious—and more likely—application would involve arson.

Arson, in the lexicon of American law, is one of those extreme offenses deemed "heinous." Some statutes list it along with attempted murder and rape as grounds for a killing response. But, speaking both practically and legally, there are certain circumstances that must prevail before the killing of the arsonist may be justified.

Again, he may not be slain after the fact: at this point, no useful purpose accrues from his death save the satisfaction of the society's need to punish or avenge. Whether this privileged responsibility belongs to God or the State, it does not belong to you.

The only situation in which you could justifiably shoot an arsonist would be if he were caught in the act of setting the fire, and refused your order to cease and desist. If he ran from the scene and you chased and shot him, you would not merely have violated the rule against slaying offenders after the crime had been committed, you would have neglected your greater duty to put out the flames, or call the fire department.

When is Lethal Force Applicable?

The classic rule is that the right of self-defense begins when the deadly danger begins, ends when the danger ends, and revives when the danger returns. As we have seen, a killing that has taken place after the threat or the crime itself cannot be claimed as self-defense, if only because at that point no real challenge remains to defend against. At the other end, violent defense is not justified a moment before the attack is about to begin.

An *advance threat* may be met with killing force only when that threat occurs immediately prior to what the slayer can reasonably anticipate will be a murderous or crippling assault against him. "Do I have to wait for my attacker to fire the first shot?" This seems to be the most common self-defense question from both police and civilians.

The answer is no. If you have real reason to believe that the man is about to commence an assault, you are fully within your rights to strike the first blow. The pre-emptory first strike is a strategy as applicable to individual conflict as to military theory.

Just when is the assailant "about to commence" his attack? The indications of the assault must take place here and now, *immediately* prior to your own active defense. Every court in the land has held that past threats do not constitute tangible jeopardy in the present. The threat must be immediate; even his actions a minute ago do not make your opponent legally subject to your deadly force.

It is time we defined the nature of the "threat." For our purposes, we are not talking of only verbal threats, but of grave and present danger *that we have good reason to believe* will immediately be translated into physical assault. Many courts have held that a cocked fist or raised bludgeon does *not* constitute deadly force—to be a killing power that calls for killing defensive power, the blow must actually be swung, if not struck. Obviously, a criminal's gun need not be fired before you can respond. It needn't even be drawn, so long as you have damn good proof that he had the weapon and was about to go for it.

When considering the oft-encountered legal rule that a punch or kick does not warrant armed defense, the practical man will do well to realize that these laws have been formulated by judges and legislators who spend their lives in the security of courtrooms and hearing chambers. It is a rare lawmaker who has ever witnessed or undergone a brutal physical assault. Those Americans who have—and who may live with the prospect every day—realize just how much damage can be done with hands and feet. A seasoned street-fighter, or even an amateur in the grip of a savage, murderous impulse, can puncture your eyeballs, crush your testicles, snap your windpipe, break your spine and cave in your skull in less time than it takes for the scream to choke in your throat.

So terrible an assault occasions a more powerful response from you than does the lesser force of simple assault and battery. The crippling or mutilating of a victim is also a greater legal degree of attack: defined as *mayhem* or *maiming*, it lies between aggravated assault and manslaughter in judicial terms of its seriousness. It will be cold comfort to the victim who has suffered paralysis, blindness, or loss of sexual powers that his assailant was convicted of mayhem and given a year's suspended sentence instead of the $25 assault fine for breaking his jaw.

Speaking practically, one cannot determine whether a punch is aimed for jaw or eye socket, or the kick intended for shin or genitals, until the blow has landed. The doctrine of "no weapons against the weaponless" exists for the good reason that it may prevent gunmen from shooting down unarmed men on the pretext of a supposed assault by the latter. At the same time, the present standard is unrealistic, and in need of alteration. Some states leave "reasonable force" open to interpretation, and some of those who do proscribe the use of guns against fists waive the consideration when the assault is particularly savage—but here again, the intensity of the attack will seldom become apparent until potentially crippling damage has been done.

Can you take your chances with a "no-gun-against-fist" law? Probably, though you'll have to go to a superior court for an acquittal if you're indicted.

I can't recommend that you violate the law as it stands in court precedent. I think I know what I'd do personally. And even if a supreme court didn't vindicate me, I wouldn't leave the courthouse in a wheelchair.

One glaring omission in the court precedents is an indicated response for knife attack. The men who make the precedents are lawyers and judges; the men who live by them are the cops and armed citizens who are likely to face deadly weapons, and one of

16

their most frequent questions is, "How close do I have to let a guy with a knife get before I can pull the trigger?"

The courts do not seem to have considered the nearness of the knife wielder required to bring his blade into deadly effect. Most decisions appear to have lumped weapon with lethal weapon, and have granted the defendant with a gun the right to shoot the attacker with a knife, period. Obviously, if the blade-man fell 25 yards from the gun muzzle, he could not be considered close enough to realistically threaten the defender's life. Perhaps because most instances of civilian self-defense occur at point-blank range, there has never been a major test case to flatly resolve this question. If it were to come up in a contemporary court, it would probably be decided in accordance with this basic self-defense doctrine: THE ATTACKER MUST NOT MERELY HAVE MADE THE THREAT TO ATTACK, BUT MUST BE IN A POSITION WHERE HE IS OBVIOUSLY AND IMMEDIATELY CAPABLE OF CARRYING OUT THAT THREAT.

Confronted with a knife-attack, therefore, you may resort to lethal force only when the attacker is close enough to take a fast running jump and put his blade through your body. He can do it starting a longer distance away than you'd think. Certainly, a man a room's length away can quickly close with you and bring his knife into effect, as any accomplished blade-fighter could testify. Beyond 25 feet, perhaps a good deal less, you'll find the judge skeptical as to whether a knife-wielder represented a present, palpable danger.

This is another basic consideration. The assailant must not only have shown that he is willing to kill or maim you: *he must be apparently able to do so at the moment you pull the trigger.* The "pre-emptive strike" concept—you get him before he gets you—applies only if he actually is near enough to get you.

Distance is, obviously, of little relevance when you're facing a remote control weapon like a gun, bow, or throwable explosive. "But he can throw the knife!" most students inject at this point in the lecture.

The distance beyond which a thrown knife ceases to be immediately dangerous is open to conjecture. There has been no definitive court opinion on the question, again probably because self-defense killings tend to occur at point-blank range. Practically speaking, the knife cannot be thrown with any effect from a hand that is wrapped around the handle in a stabbing or slashing position. To hurl a knife with accuracy and penetrating power, the blade or handle must be grasped at one end or the other (not always in the by-the-tip position seen on TV). The weight and balance must be just right; switchblades and pocket stilettos have rotten balance, and are too light for good throwing. But even a jackknife can be thrown true at a surprising distance by a sharp-eyed man who knows what he's doing, and is having a good day.

If you shoot a knife-armed attacker while he is still some distance away from you, the issue will probably be settled in your own court, by your own standards. Use your own judgment as to how close the blade must be to reach you. But judge carefully: a smart prosecutor who really wanted to hang you could take this question and make a dramatic demonstration in front of the jury, designed to show how the deceased couldn't possibly have thrown the knife accurately from any great distance. Something like challenging you to throw the decedent's knife at a set-up target, would exemplify the kind of courtroom showmanship that can sway juries away from practical considerations.

How would one counter a spectacle such as that? Personally, I would contact one of those groups of history-buffs who collect old-time firearms and edged weapons. Not only do they have regular competition with their black-powder rifles, but tomahawk and bowie-knife throwing matches as well are included in their tests of mountain man skills. The deftness with which they can impale a coin or other small object on the heavy blade at incredible distances would certainly be an impressive demonstration that a knife can be deadly far beyond arm's reach.

A razor, however, can't be considered deadly much more than a couple of paces beyond the length of the arm.

One practical consideration to remember when you're facing a knife: Don't think your opponent has to raise his arm in the classic stance before throwing it. A knife can be tossed underhand or sidehand with deadly accuracy and force.

Where does that leave you on the question of distance? In the absence of a legal opinion, my own is that anyone a home-size room away with a knife can kill me with it. I'd worry less about a throw than a sudden lunge: as we will see in the gunfighting chapters, no handgun can be counted on to drop a man in his tracks.

As we have seen, one has the greatest latitude in choosing to employ killing power when he responds to attack in his home. Almost the same applies when attacked in one's place of business, or in the home of a host; only rarely will retreat be required in any of these places.

On the street, the need to retreat may be obviated by circumstances—for instance, the suddenness or savagery of attack, or the hopelessness of retreat from a position where trying to run would only make you as or more vulnerable than if you stood your ground. Statutes of the given jurisdiction may allow you to stand fast, whether or not flight would weaken your position to protect yourself.

Bare Fear and Reasonable Fear

All courts will hold, by statute or by logic, that "bare fear" does not warrant deadly force. *While the attacker need not actually be about to kill or maim you, or another party you are justified to protect, you must have sound reason to believe he is* before you pull the trigger.

What are the essential grounds for assuming that you are dealing with a threat of lethal force?

Let us first dispense with the obvious: an armed or even unarmed man in the act of savage attack is a free target for his intended victim, or the victim's rescuers. So is any assailant in the act of murderous or potentially crippling assault against an innocent party. What "bare fear" concerns is the interpretation of such danger when the nature of the criminal attack is not entirely evident, or when it has not quite yet taken place.

As we have seen, the citizen may smite the criminal at the moment he realizes the criminal is himself about to strike. At what point the intent to make a criminal assault becomes evident is determined by the doctrine of *reasonable apprehension*, or the validity of the belief that an attack is imminent.

The indications of that belief are many and varied. The simple fact that the assailant says, "I'm going to kill/maim/rape you" is not sufficient grounds; he must have the physical wherewithal, and the close physical proximity to the victim, to carry out that threat. *And it must appear that he is actually going to.* His saying, "I have a gun" does not prove that he has one and will use it, and therefore does not justify the use of yours. A sudden reach to the pocket or under the coat, in the manner of one going for a weapon, *does* justify your use of deadly force.

So does an unarmed physical attack, under certain circumstances. Suppose you are minding your own business and an assailant walks up to you, grabs you by the throat, and punches you in the face. You can't shoot him yet; he has not offered a sufficient show of deadly force.

Suppose, after punching you, he snarls, "You sonofabitch, I'll kill you." You still can't use deadly force, *unless he is so powerful and has you in such a compromising position that he can carry out his threat if he has a mind to.* Here, you have more latitude. He has shown all the necessary requirements for your homicidal response: he has voiced the intention to harm you gravely, and has struck the initial blow of a potentially deadly assault. He has you at close, inescapable quarters—by the throat. You are an innocent party. In most jurisdictions, unless there are mitigating circumstances, the justification for protective homicide now exists.

What if, in the past, he has threatened you, or even beat hell out of you? In and of itself, this is meaningless. Past incidents are no cause for present killing. But if it is this man who is submitting you to the previously-described assault, you have added cause to respond with potent force. While the previous instance does not pertain directly to the present assault, it can be considered relevant in that it has given you a concrete reason to fear your assailant, and to consider him capable of carrying out his violent threat. The fact that he may be, in general, a vicious and unsavory person does not in and of itself give you any advantage—the law states specifically that the bad man is protected by the same rights and safeties as the good. But the fact that he has previously assaulted *you* gives you reasonable ground to believe that he harbors sufficient animosity against you that his carrying out the threat is a matter of certainty, and you are all the more justified in terminating the assault by gunfire.

If, however, there is no actual present assault, and the previous instance alone is your only indication of his deadly intent, you are *not* justified in killing him. Never cause in itself for killing, personal knowledge of the attacker's propensity for violence toward you or others is often not even admissible as evidence or testimony. Only as a reason for your believing that a deadly assault was about to take place—and only if other circumstances indicate the same—will it be taken into the consideration of the court.

Bare fear, then, can sometimes be the misinterpretation of past episodes as cause for present defense. An even clearer example is when apprehension of attack rises from the mere presence of a stranger or group of strangers, without any reasonable indication that an assault is in the offing. For instance, an individual walks past a group of tough-looking persons on a street corner. One of them, perhaps, makes a snotty remark.

"Oh my God, they're going to get me," panics the individual, going for his gun. He is at this moment in the grip of bare fear—a morbid fantasy without basis in fact, on the grounds of which he is about to wrongly employ lethal force.

Bare fear is generally considered to be the mark of the paranoiac and the abject coward. It is the difference between, "He is about to assault me!" and "What if he assaults me?"

Innocence

A cornerstone of a legitimate claim of self-defense is the innocence of the claimant. He must be entirely without fault. If he has begun the conflict or quarrel, or if he has kept it going or escalated it when it lay in his power to abort it before it became a killing situation, he shares a degree of culpability.

The self-defense plea, in this case, will not be allowed. The killing is, legally, neither justifiable nor excusable. The court will probably find you guilty of manslaughter, unless it is shown that you deliberately provoked the encounter with the intention of killing the deceased. In this event, you have premeditated a first-degree murder. An associated consideration is "good faith," that, is, your endeavor throughout the incident to avoid using any more force than you had to. If it can be proven that, even though you were free of malice at the start you decided somewhere midpoint in the struggle, "I'm going to kill this sonofabitch, no matter what," your protection under the law of self-defense has ceased as of that moment.

There are instances where both combatants share equal blame. Most states still carry on their books laws pertaining to duels. When two men deliberately enter into mortal combat of their own free will, the survivor is automatically chargeable with first-degree murder. A modern-day counterpart of the situation these laws were meant for would be a "let's go out in the alley" brawl fought with deadly weapons instead of fists and feet.

An interesting variation of the self-defense concept is that which applies when two men are cast into a crisis where one man could survive the peril, but not both. The classic example is a pair of shipwrecked sailors clinging to a floating spar that can only support one of them. The one who drowns the other is the winner by a verdict of justifiable homicide and the Law of Survival both.

A contemporary example is brought to mind by the recently publicized news stories of plane-wreck victims who survived for months until rescued from their foodless wastelands. In the past, such incidents were called "miracles of deliverance." Today's straight-mouthed press called it what it was: morally justified cannibalism. Every authority from the law to the highest arms of the church condoned these acts. It would have been interesting to see their response had it proven that the weaker survivors had not expired naturally before being devoured.

The fear of being cut off from his artificial food supply lines is one that exists deep inside every civilized man. It is one of the recurring nightmares that some thriller writers have exploited in the "lost in the lifeboat" genre of movies and short stories. That the gruesome ultimate consequence of such situations has only today gained the acknowledged approval of the world is, perhaps, a sign of the times.

Escalation

The concept of *escalation of force* is rarely encountered in the study of self-defense law, and then not as such. There are only the general references to equality or reciprocity of force.

Escalation is perhaps the only deadly force theory to evolve as much in the street as in the courtroom. It has been developed over the years by the last of the professional gunfighters, the police officers of the special felony squads that deal exclusively with violent crime.

Sgt. Joseph Volpato, then Acting Commander of the NYCPD Stakeout Unit, explained escalation to me in this manner: "When our men make a confrontation (with armed robbers at the crime scene), there is always an escalation of force. First, the officers identify themselves, and order the gunmen to drop their weapons. If they turn on us with guns, we have no choice but to shoot; we have to assume that they are turning for the purpose of shooting at us. We do not aim specifically to wound or to kill, but to stop.

"This is our standard procedure. We always follow this pattern of escalation, even if things break so fast that it occurs in the space of a second."

It's a good pattern. It has to be, for a couple of reasons. First, every shooting of a criminal in New York is investigated thoroughly. Any hint of impropriety, i.e., shooting a suspect before it was warranted, would reflect badly on the Unit.

Second, and perhaps more important is the personal consideration of each man involved. The stake-out unit faced armed robbers exclusively, every one of whom is prepared to kill a cop or anyone else who would stop them. They often try.

Consequently, the 40-man unit got into more gunfights in a year than almost any whole department in the country. Some of the men had to kill as many as five or six gunmen, either in straight shootouts or as the bandits were about to murder shopkeepers. That many kills can be hard to live with. While a combat soldier's philosophy pervades the squad, the men admit that they couldn't sleep at night if they didn't *know* they were justified in taking those lives, justified even *beyond* the letter of the law.

This, then, is why they adopted an SOP of giving a gunman a chance to surrender when, legally, they could probably gun them down from ambush the minute the hoods pulled their weapons.

Escalation for Civilians

Do you, the private citizen, have to go to that point? Actually, no. Neither do stakeout cops, for that matter, and but for their superb, regularly-practiced marksmanship and the fact that they are selected for coolness under stress, they probably wouldn't come so close to giving the first shot away to their opponent. You, of course, *can't* allow that much leeway for the sake of making the justifiability of the act more plain than, perhaps, required. What the civilian can learn from the stakeout squad's format of escalation is a pattern that is both legal and moral, yet thoroughly practical when properly undertaken.

Notice that two civilian fantasies of gunfighting are not present: the warning shot and the shot to wound.

I recommend warning shots only for police, and only to halt a fleeing felon, and then only under certain circumstances. A civilian has no need to fire warning shots when the criminal is attacking him—indeed, it will only cost him a precious moment and a precious cartridge. If he has justification to shoot, he should shoot to stop; if deadly force is not warranted, the gun should remain silent, period.

A shot to wound is foolish. You should shoot at a human being only if he is about to kill or cripple you or another; if that degree of danger is imminent, you cannot afford to trifle with it by counter-assaulting with only enough force to slow down, rather than stop, the felonious attack.

Also, few civilians realize just how much damage a non-fatal wound can create. Generations of watching screen stars treat shoulder wounds like scratches, and barely limp after stopping a bullet in the leg, have given Joe Citizen the idea that the "shot to wound" is little more than a sort of remote control punch. This is far from true.

A high powered bullet through the complex of shoulder bones and muscles will leave the arm crippled for life. The same with a leg. The possibility of death from hemorrhage or shock is present with *any* bullet wound. A bullet in the side or abdomen can fatally damage liver, kidneys, and other organs. People don't always recover completely from serious gunshot wounds, even if they do survive initially. Damage can be lingering—"he was never any good after he was shot" is a common description—and the results of the wound can radically shorten the natural life span. Remember, if he dies of the wound or complications thereof within a year and a day, it's legally the same as if he died outright at the shooting scene.

And if you weren't qualified to use killing force, woe unto you if you make a "shot-to-wound" that maims in this fashion. For one thing, ask your attorney how much more a crippled man can sue the causer for than can the family of the deceased.

The very fact that you did not "shoot to kill" can indicate that you did not consider the crisis a killing situation; it could be decided that your degree of response was more than you, even at the time, reasonably believed was necessary.

What will perhaps be remembered as the definitive guideline of street practicality in this area, is this advice from a savvy old

Border Patrolman (and firearms authority and gunfight veteran) to less experienced cops: ". . . in establishing the amount of force which was necessary, you will probably find it easier to convince a coroner's jury that you didn't shoot him too much than that you didn't hit him too hard."[3]

He was talking about clubbing suspects with the service revolver, but the principle applies to any attempt to inflict non-lethal injury with an inherently lethal weapon.

A specific example of practical escalation is seen in the chapter, "A Gun on the Street." Escalation of force, then, is a precise, practical approach to the legal doctrine of reciprocal response in self-defense. For the civilian it means, when time and the heat of the moment permit, that there should be a verbal warning to the assailant, but neither a warning shot nor a shot aimed to disable. If the warning is ignored, or cannot be issued without jeopardizing the defender or the innocent party about to be slain or badly injured, the situation has escalated. It has reached the point where the degree of preventative force that is justifiable now encompasses the right to kill.

---

[3]Jordan, William H., "No Second Place Winner"; Shreveport, 1967.

Chapter 3
The Dangerous Myth of Citizen's Arrest

Most folks have a vague idea that, under certain extreme circumstances, they can make something called a citizen's arrest.

Actually, the laws generally state that the private citizen who witnesses a felony is authorized to place the suspect under arrest. In some states, this right is extended to cope with misdemeanors. Citizen's arrest in the latter case usually involves an arm-chair policeman who loves to pull over speeders and whatnot.

While many states do not separate police from civilians in their laws of lethal force, most do. Generally speaking, the private party has much less practical arrest power than the sworn peace-officer, statutory authority sometimes to the contrary.

As far as the use of lethal force by the citizen arrester, justification for this is usually limited to (a) such time as he is assisting a sworn officer and uses that force at the officer's express command, or (b) when in the course of rendering that assistance, he is faced with the kind of grave and immediate threat that would normally justify a citizen's use of killing force anyway.

It is the first circumstance that can be tricky. First off, if the sworn officer either did not have the authority to order the shooting, or acted wrongly in giving the command, the citizen arrestor's degree of guilt in the erroneous shooting will vary from state to state. Some specifically excuse him from carrying out the officer's bad judgment so long as he had reason to believe that the officer had the authority to give the command, so long as he acted in good faith in pulling the trigger, and so long as there was no evidence plain to him that would contradict the cop's order. However, other states, in making provision for the use of lethal force by citizen arrestors acting in the assistance of regular police, specifically exempt from justification shootings occasioned by an erroneous command from the officer in charge.

Speaking in practical rather than legal terms, you are on thin ice any time you pull the trigger on the basis of anyone else's judgment. Even if the command comes from a sworn officer, even if his judgment was correct, it is always possible that you could misinterpret his orders.

Cops aren't used to working with untrained civilians. When one of them shouts a warning or command to a brother officer, he knows he is talking to a man who is fully, professionally aware of the boundaries of his authority. If a fleeing suspect has outpaced him but is within reach of his partner, he doesn't cry, "Stop that person's flight with all reasonable and necessary force." He yells, "Get him!"

A man with a gun, lawfully pursuing a fugitive, feels an impulse to shoot that must be resisted despite the excitement of the moment. Civilians, who generally don't carry guns eight hours a day or receive several hours of justifiable force instruction, tend to be awfully bloodthirsty. The situation is understandable. The private citizen assisting a policeman does, in good faith, what he thinks a policeman is supposed to do. His only learning models are the policemen he sees on the screen, who shoot running suspects with impunity. (I remember the scene in "The French Connection" where the detective kills the underworld enforcer at the subway station. The episode begins when the gunsel tries to kill the detective with a sniper rifle from a rooftop, and shoots a couple of bystanders instead. He escapes through the subway, which the detective follows by car in a chilling chase scene. By the time he catches up with the gunman, the latter has shot down two innocent people, and caused a train wreck in which he has lost his gun. When detective Popeye Doyle confronts the now-unarmed criminal, who turns to run, Doyle puts a bullet through his spine.

The audience cheered. They didn't seem to realize that the cop couldn't have known what the fugitive had done on the subway train. It didn't register that the cop couldn't have positively identified the suspect from the quick glimpse he'd had of the sniper on the. rooftop, or that he had undertaken the pursuit without attempting to help the wounded bystanders. The theater-goers cheered anyway, and the only people in the audience who didn't join in were the off-duty cops.)

It is a widespread and dangerous misconception that all criminals are fair game for the bullets of good guys. A basic principle of American justice holds that a bad man has the same rights as a good man. When the pursuer lets his own sense of justice determine whether the chased is a man with the same rights as his, or a target of opportunity, the stage has been set for tragedy.

Let us return to our hypothetical case, the armed citizen assisting a police officer in the apprehension of a suspect. The cop yells, "Get him!" The citizen aims his gun and pulls the trigger. Seconds later, they are both standing over the corpse of an unarmed man who, perhaps, had committed a felony of minor proportions, "My God," gasps the cop, "I didn't tell you to *shoot* him!" If the dead man's survivors sue the community, they may stand a chance of winning, no matter what the statutes say about fleeing felons. More important will be the response of the press: if the citizen has shot down an unarmed youth trying only to get away, he has put himself in a most unsavory position. The police department involved will not find it in its own interest to endorse the act, or worse, to suggest that it occurred at the command of the local police authority.

The citizen in question has committed an act beyond his own legal power. A police officer who did the same would probably be roasted by the press and community, and would have only the specific statutory authority to shield him from charges, if that. Even if the statutes give the assisting civilian the same "shoot-to-stop" power, a jury simply won't see it in that light, in every case.

Neither will the cop involved. Remember, he said "Get him," not "Shoot him." The fact that the citizen arrester did not understand the limitations of his informally deputized power buys him nothing; ignorance is no defense in the eyes of the law.

Where does this leave the citizen who shot the running suspect he thought was *supposed* to be shot? It leaves him on his own, fighting what may be a sea of angry public opinion and the resentment of a police department that has been made to look bad by an amateur who, in their view, went beyond his powers in assisting the police and took the law into his own hands.

The policeman who makes an error in judgment has, at least, the sympathy and support of his own professional community. The other cops know that, but for the grace of God, it would have been them who had wound up in that unenviable position. Cops take a lot of shit from ordinary people and punks alike; they tend to become insular and self-protective. They look out for their own and despise people who make them look bad. The citizen who has over-ridden his bounds of cop-assisting arrest power can look for support only from these people whom he has embarrassed and offended. And far from sharing in the protective society of the law-enforcement group, he has now thoroughly alienated it.

He who chooses to play the role of Citizen Cop does so at his own peril. A man requested by a police officer to assist the latter must do so, on pain of being a convicted obstructor of justice. But he owes it to himself to watch out for his own interests before those of the law or the community. Confronted with a fleeing felon, it is in the citizen arrester's best interests to hold his fire. The question of whether he is responsible for the escaped suspect's future crimes is less imminent and painful than the probability that he will be crucified for using more force than he should have. He must consider every repercussion that his every response could create, in light of laws and public opinion that will damn him the moment he steps out of bounds.

In short, the citizen arrester must cope with an intensified form of the socio-legal threat that every full-fledged police officer faces every hour of his working day.

A final caution: The legal protection offered to the man who is assisting an officer goes into effect *only when the officer asks you to assist him*. The man who is just driving by, witnesses a pursuit, and joins in, will not be considered a volunteer police officer. If anything happens, he'll be seen as a show-off who interrupted police business and caused a tragedy. *Offer* to assist, if you wish, but never join in without being specifically asked. And *always* go easy on the trigger finger.

And never forget that support officers racing in to assist may mistake you for the bad guy and blow you up. "Oops," as we say in the trade.

Making the Arrest

The first thing that occurs to the private party contemplating citizen's arrest is, "Do I have to give him his Constitutional rights?"

Let us first consider whether you have arrested him. Contrary to popular belief, it is not necessary to say, "You're my prisoner" or something such, for the man to be under arrest; in most states, arrest takes place as soon as you take a person into custody and detain him from leaving the scene.

What you are doing, really, is holding him for the police. As soon as they pick him up they'll read him his rights whether you did or not.

The only time the rights would come into question would be if his conviction rested on some confession or other statement given to you between when you apprehended him and when you turned him over. It's likely that your testimony as to what you observed, which caused you to detain him, will be a lot more important in gaining a conviction.

"The rights," to be valid, are too long to be memorized by most people. The versions you hear on TV are usually shortened for fear that the whole narration will put viewers to sleep. Cops read them from cards when making an arrest. A sample "rights card" reads,

I am a police officer (and the officer introduces himself and others that may be present, if any). I warn you that anything you do or say may be used in a court of law against you. You have an absolute right to remain silent and you have the right of advice of a lawyer before questioning, and the presence of a lawyer, here with you during questioning and that if you cannot afford a lawyer, one will be appointed for you free before any questioning. If you decide to talk to me, you may stop answering questions any time you wish. You are entitled to make a phone call. Do you fully understand what I have just told you? Do you want a lawyer present? (Yes or no.)

Two problems. Cops give the rights to disarmed, handcuffed suspects; *your* captive has his hands free and would like nothing better than for you to flick your eyes down to read off a rights card. *NEVER take your eyes off a man you're holding at gunpoint.*

Secondly, when you come to the part where you say, "Do you understand these rights," your captive may say, "No, I don't, fuckface. Suppose you explain it to me." Since you probably can't explain without giving him misinformation, you may as well have kept your mouth shut the whole time.

Altogether, it's just as well to forget about "reading the rights" in a citizen's arrest. Think of yourself as a citizen holding a suspect for police, not as a self-appointed arresting officer.

As far as identifying yourself, don't impersonate a police officer. At the same time, if you're ordering a man to stop, yell, "Police! Hold it!" If anyone asks, you can say later that you were shouting for the police in the same breath that you ordered the suspect to halt. How fast is he going to stop if you cry, "Hold it! Private Citizen"? The cry will also prevent your being mistaken for a fleeing felon by officers arriving on the scene.

If you really want to be able to arrest somebody, see about becoming a special officer in your local department. Besides, if you ever are involved in a shooting, it doesn't hurt to be referred to as "an off-duty policeman."

Chapter 4
Samaritans
With Guns

On a warm summer night in 1963, a young girl was slowly stabbed to death on a residential street in New York as anywhere from 38 to over 200 witnesses looked and listened and turned away. It was an incident that shocked a nation, and made "Don't get involved" a byword for the urban American life style.

In the decade that followed, it became increasingly apparent that Kitty Genovese's death was not an isolated nightmare, though she would remain the first recognized martyr to the collective apathy of the American citizen.

The situation has been repeated again and again, and in the small towns and hinterlands as well as the cities. The only places where one can still count on a by-stander's assistance are Alaska and some parts of the rural South and Southwest. It is not a coincidence that these are the same areas where it is common for the average citizen to carry a gun on his person or in his car. The refusal to even call police or assist an injured or stricken victim when there is no longer any danger to the rescuer, is a phenomenon I will leave to the analysis of better philosophers than I. But the refusal of an unarmed man to physically intervene in a one-sided act of violence is understandable.

Not long ago, a cabdriver who attempted to rescue an elderly victim from a gang of muggers was shot in the head by one of the attackers. It was an object lesson to the other members of the community that they, too, could lose their lives in an unarmed rescue attempt—in this case, at the hands of the selfsame 16-year-old punk who shot the cabdriver. He had been freed by a court which decided that the failure to inform him that he would be tried as an adult, was a violation of his constitutional rights.

Nor is the armed citizen altogether free to intervene with deadly force in an assault involving others. For instance, he cannot always tell who is the guilty party, and who is the victim: what if the latter has managed to overpower his assailant at the moment the potential rescuer comes on the scene?

Legally, some states permit the citizen to use the same force to save a third party that the latter could use himself if he were able. The other lethal force doctrines are the same: death or great bodily harm to an innocent party must be imminent and unavoidable. However, other states permit you to kill only to protect yourself, or a member of your immediate family or household.

If you intervene in a street assault, be *really* sure where you and everyone else stands. *Never* use a gun on a purse-snatcher, pickpocket, shoplifter, or car thief. *Never* pursue a fleeing felon unless you are assisting a police officer who has specifically asked you for your help. And *never* shoot a running man unless he has committed a cop-killing, a savage, malicious mutilation, or crime of similar magnitude before your very eyes, and has done so in such a manner as to convince a reasonable man that he is a grave and present danger to the general public so long as he remains at large. Even in this instance, you can make a tragic error: he may be a terrified victim who has just turned the tables on a mugger, kicked in his head in a frenzy of panic, and run away instinctively.

Chapter 5
Women and Guns

The view of most women toward self-defense is a pathetic paradox. They are discouraged from using deadly weapons, yet the need for effective protection is there, now more than ever as the crime rate grows, and that need is well recognized. A frequent theme in women's magazines is "How to Protect Yourself From Rape" (or mugging, or housebreaking, etc.). The articles are all a rehash of the same suggestions, the same pathetic, inadequate defenses that must, it seems, have been conceived by laymen and journalists.

They tell you, the woman, that all manner of innocuous household items will save you from brutal physical attack by person or persons much larger and stronger than you, from persons motivated by demented inner demons that neither you nor, in all probability, the writers of these articles can possibly imagine.

Let us examine, first, the traditional "female weapons." One is the venerable hatpin. The magazines are fond of telling you solemnly that these little instruments can kill. And so they can, in an Alfred Hitchcock mystery when somebody uses one to do in Aunt Agatha in the midst of her afternoon nap. A hatpin against a mugger? In real life, it's as hopeless and ridiculous as it sounds.

"Carry a police whistle," they tell you in the magazines. In many parts of the country, the sound of a police signal would only be a call to shut the windows and check the bolts on the doors. Besides, the cops won't hear you except in the unlikely event that one is walking a beat nearby. Police coverage being as sparse as it is everywhere, and with late-night foot patrols almost a thing of the past, that would take a miracle.

"Scream your head off, and he'll run like a rabbit." The moment you open your mouth, a seasoned mugger will chop you across the throat.

"Carry a pepper shaker to throw in his face." Great. He'll sneeze the whole time he's raping you, and you can tell the police to look for a man with a red nose.

" . . . a pointy umbrella." Such a makeshift weapon combines the worst features of bludgeon and spear. It is incapable of inflicting a deterring puncture wound, unless the tip has been sharpened. Used as a club, it has neither weight nor speed enough to deliver a stunning blow. It comprises the techniques of the sword, the lance, and the bludgeon—all of which require great physical strength to be effective.

"... a steak knife in your pocketbook." Actually *worse* than useless. A knife requires speed and skill: unless you have the coordination of a ballerina and the special weapons training of a Green Beret, your knife will be taken away from you in a matter of moments. If you have managed to take a small slice out of your attacker, you've done little more than make him mean. Besides, most good defense knives are illegal to carry.

"You should kick him where it hurts." No way. Your assailant is waiting for you to do just that if he knows anything about attacking women or fighting in the street. The moment you take one foot off the ground you'll probably wind up on your back.

"... jab his eyes." Another standard ploy he'll be braced for. A V-fingered jab can be deflected by a flick of the head; if you claw at his eyes with your hands and thumbs, he's liable to break your arms.

"... or learn karate." Judo and karate are great fighting techniques to one who develops and practices them, but their value to the amateur has been grossly exaggerated. A 110-pound woman with karate background has a better chance against a 200-pound mugger than if she had no training—but she's still a 110-pound woman against a 200-pound man.

(Actually, judo and karate are great forms of exercise, since they give you a fun incentive to keep it up. But don't expect miracles of defensive capability.)

"Or maybe Chemical Mace." For one thing, you can't get real Mace (a product of Smith & Wesson that has become a generic term for all incapacitating aerosols). The strong formulas are sold only to police, and watered-down stuff to civilians. Since the complaints about suspects' eye damage in the mid-Sixties, all formulas have been weakened across the board.

The Mace-type sprays have proven to be much less effective than once believed. Many people can take several streams of the stuff square in the face with no immediate ill effects. It only works right off when it's sprayed in the eyes, which is a no-no. Even that

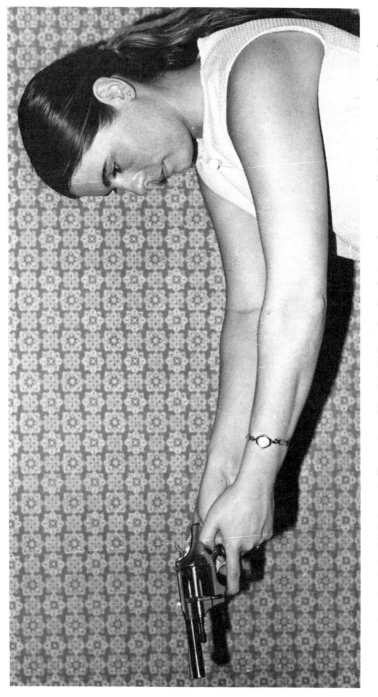

.22 revolver loaded with Stinger hollowpoints, like this Hi-Standard 9-shot, can be an excellent defense gun choice for women.

won't work if your assailant wears glasses, or shades. Drunks are almost immune. The instructions say to spray at the chest, so he'll inhale the rising fumes. It just doesn't work that way.

The police department to which I am attached issues Curb 60, the most potent such spray. On one occasion, I was accidentally sprayed in the face with it. I had sense enough not to inhale, but wiped off as much as I could and held my breath as I walked to the nearest sink to flush the exposed skin. There was a tingling that began after a few moments, and grew to a burning sensation like very strong after-shave before I washed the stuff off. I did have some trouble breathing, but nothing incapacitating.

Forget Mace. The only thing it's good for is to facilitiate rape (sprayed into the victim's face, she can't breath enough to scream or resist), or to cope with vicious dogs (susceptible only because the mucous membranes of their tongues and noses are directly exposed to the spray).

"But police advise you not to buy a gun." That's how all those articles end, with an explanation that you'll shoot yourself instead of the attacker.

It's bullshit, all bullshit. Guns are the only weapons that put a physically small or weak person at parity with a powerful, very possibly armed, criminal.

Learning to Shoot

Women pick up firearms training much faster than men, just as rookies learn quicker than veterans. It's probably because there's no subconscious resentment at being taught something by another man that you, in your own sex or occupational role, are supposed to know already. Some women do feel it's expected of them to act skittish and dainty around guns, but very few continue to be cutesy-poo after the training is under way.

You should learn to grip the weapon in both hands, deliberately line up the sights, and squeeze the trigger until the gun goes off. Become thoroughly familiar with it, preferably under the tutelage of certified instructors. Actually, your learning procedure will differ little from that described in the gunfighting chapter.

Choice of Weapons

As with a man, the best quality you can afford, and the most powerful you can handle is your optimum weapon. Forget der-

With solid 2-hand hold, even petite women can master guns like this .38 Special snubnose.

ringers, or those classic "lady's guns," the tiny .25 automatics. They're too hard to shoot straight, and too weak to stop an assailant unless you hit him just right. It's really an expert's weapon, not for the amateurs.

.45's and Magnums are too powerful for small hands to control. .32's don't have enough stopping power, and there's still some kick. A .380 automatic, or a 2" or 3" barrel .38 Special loaded with light, fast-moving bullets, generally represent about the maximum.

A .22 revolver or automatic firing the long rifle hollow point cartridge may be a novice woman's best bet. Stopping power is more than the .25's, but still unspectacular. The only advantages are the ease of practice with cheap ammo; the fact that it's not so loud when it goes off in an enclosed space to paralyze her with terror; and the fact that most women like .22's and avoid bigger guns. If it's comfortable for you, that's worth a lot. For the same reasons, a .22 pistol often makes the best defense gun for an elderly person.

If you do work up to a .38, lean *way* forward into the recoil, unless you're a big girl.

Women and Deadly Force

It is probably true that women are much more reluctant to use grave physical force than are men. It is equally true that they can, given sufficient provocation, be driven to extremes of homicidal assault. We men like to talk about how the women of the tribe are always the ones who torture the prisoners and what not.

Still, women have a certain native timidity. You often hear, "Oh, I'd scare him away with the gun, but I could never really *shoot* any body."

ANYONE who really feels this way should abandon any thoughts of keeping guns. A criminal can tell when a person isn't going to shoot, the way a dog can smell fear. And to pull a gun you don't intend to use is to flaunt a power you do not really command: you are inviting the opponent to take it away from you, and antagonizing him to use it against you.

Female responses to deadly threat are funny. A woman who would suffer indignity, mutilation, or death rather than take a life, might tear the throat out of an intruder who approached her baby's crib. But the will and ability to use the defense gun in the

40

ultimate defense must be there always. If they aren't, the men who wrote those articles were right: the gun kept for protection really is more likely to be turned on you than on a criminal.

Where to Carry

The woman who carries a gun is faced with a practical problem not shared by her male counterpart: she has no place to put the thing. The handbag has been the standard location ever since hand muffs went out of style.

You'll have a bitch of a time getting a gun out of a handbag in a hurry, though. There is always the possibility of the bag getting lost or snatched. Also, you're constantly setting it down in the course of the day, and therefore leaving it in reach of small, unauthorized hands.

You are better off to carry it on your person—if you can find a place. Women's fashions lack the pockets, belts, and constantly-worn jackets that give men places to discreetly wear sidearms. There is, for instance, no good way to carry a gun while wearing a dress. You would have to add a leather (*not* cloth) belt at least 1¼" wide, and don a sweater to cover the holster.

Bianchi had a brassierre/shoulder holster for small guns. I can't comment on it from experience, but it *looked* awfully uncomfortable.

The inside-waistband holsters would seem to be the answer with most ensembles that have either a jacket, a sweater, or an untucked blouse. Get one that holds in place with a clip, like Bianchi's. You will need to wear a full slip, or tube top, however; the sharp edges of most handguns are inhospitable to soft, bare tummies.

Chapter 6
How and When to Use Firearms in your Store

In recent years, as the rate of armed robbery and related crimes of violence has multiplied, more and more holdup-prone retailers have armed their establishments with guns.

Regrettably, many of these people are dangerously unfamiliar with firearms, and unaware of the legal, ethical and practical aspects of keeping or using them in a place of business open to the public.

The average manager or storeowner who keeps one or more guns on the premises has probably acquired them with a vague view toward "self-defense" and "security." All too many people think of guns in terms of blanket protection, when in fact their application for security purposes is very narrow and limited. The best defenses against robbery are locks, alarms, insurance, and a sensible company policy on holdups, stressing calmness and cooperation on the part of the employees during such incidents. The only purpose of the gun should be to protect oneself, store personnel and customers from the wanton violence of a drugged, psychotic, panic-stricken or simply vicious armed robber who can be restrained in no other way.

Let us consider first the circumstances under which the lethal force of a gun may be justified. The private citizen is permitted by law to employ deadly force only when he or other innocent parties are in *imminent and unavoidable danger of death or grave bodily harm.*

If you kill or cripple a felon, you will find that the burden of proof rests upon you to convince a judge or jury that there was no reasonable alternative for you except pulling the trigger; if you fail, you may be plunged into a legal nightmare from which you may emerge defamed, imprisoned, or penniless.

If, for example, you shoot a fleeing robber in the back, the court might conclude that the danger had passed when you fired, the criminal having taken flight, and that therefore the homicide you

43

have committed was not justifiable. The verdict might be excusable homicide, implying that you acted recklessly and negligently, but without malice; some in this situation have been convicted of manslaughter or worse.

Or, consider the case of a jeweler with a pistol that has not been properly registered, who kills a gunman: the slaying itself is justifiable, but the possession of the unregistered gun by the jeweler may be a felony; he has killed a man while committing a felony, and therefore can technically be charged with first degree murder.

In a few states, the citizen is privileged to use deadly force to protect his property. This is a tricky legal concept, however; a storeowner who slays a thief in one part of the country may be cited for heroism, while one who does the same elsewhere may be sentenced to prison for manslaughter or murder. Another important concept is "disparity of force"—that is, you cannot use a gun against an unarmed attacker unless he is physically much stronger than you and bent on serious injury, or unless he is one of a gang of assailants.

If you keep arms in the store, consult your attorney to determine what laws govern your possession of concealed, loaded firearms, and to what extent your state allows their use in self-defense. Your lawyer can also tell you the disposition of local courts toward such cases. Contact your insurance agent to see what your liability policy covers in this regard, for if you initiate an exchange of shots that maims a bystander, the resultant lawsuits could ruin you.

Even if you are allowed to shoot for the sole purpose of protecting your property, you must contemplate the moral aspect of doing so. It has been many years since a civilized Western nation decreed a death penalty for stealing.

If one thinks about it, killing strictly to maintain one's own material goods is not so very far removed from slaying another to gain his. And you *will* think about it. The taking of a human life is an emotionally shattering act; a normal person who terminates a fellow man's existence suffers second only to the deceased and his loved ones. You will see the latter at the coroner's inquest, and if you do not know in your heart that you *had* to shoot, you will see their faces in your sleep for the rest of your life.

Suppose, now, that you do find yourself in a situation where you

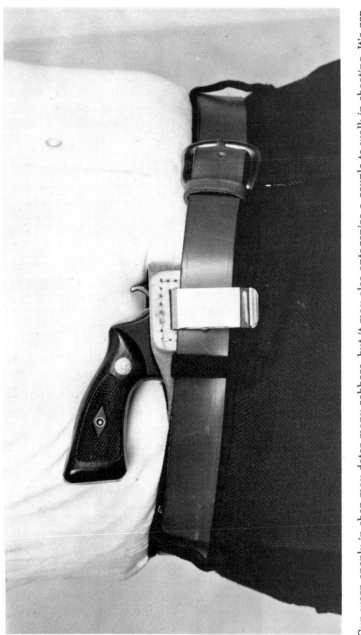

Gun worn openly in shop may deter many robbers, but it may also antagonize a couple to walk in shooting. It's generally bad strategy.

are in immediate danger of being shot—that is, you are at gunpoint. To draw against a drawn gun is suicide; this is the most basic tenet of gunfighting, not to mention common sense, yet storeowners continue to die in this foolhardy attempt. A handful have succeeded, but only because their opponents were more careless and incompetent than they. In most instances your chances of survival are better if you do not resist, for the armed robber is perhaps the most dangerous and volatile of criminals, and you must assume that he is prepared to kill at the least provocation.

There is no denying, however, that jewelers and their employees and customers have lost their lives to deranged criminals, partly because they were helpless to fight back at their armed murderers. Slight as it is, the possibility of such an atrocity is perhaps the only really valid reason for keeping a loaded gun in the store.

If you choose to keep deadly weapons in your place of business, be certain to understand the serious responsibilities attendant to the practice. Chief among these is to keep your guns out of incompetent hands. They must be neither visible nor accessible to unauthorized personnel. Customers' and employees' children tend to find their way behind counters and into back rooms—so do criminals. At the same time, since the gun is there for extreme emergencies, it must be instantly available to you and to authorized employees. You have a choice of two approaches: placing the guns at selected stationary points, or carrying one on your person.

It is impossible to get a gun quickly out of a closed drawer, including the one in your cash register. Besides, a thief might decide to personally clean out the latter. Forget open drawers or shelves under counters, in back rooms, or in the safe (a stickup man is likely to be looking over your shoulder when you open it).

A better way is to secure the gun in a holster attached to the underside of a shelf or the ceiling of a small safe, where it is hidden from anyone who doesn't know it is there. You can also nail a holster to the side of a showcase; this is a very handy place, but usually visible to anyone behind the counter. To be assured that you will have one within reach when you need it, you must store handguns in at least two strategic locations—for example, one in the safe and one near the register.

The best solution is to carry the gun on you, where it is at once instantly available and secure from undesirable hands. A gun in a pocket is slow to draw, uncomfortable, and bulgingly obvious. Don't wear shoulder holsters, which require uncomfortable harnesses, or cross-draw styles, which hold the gun in such a way that an assailant grappling with you can easily snatch it.

The best is a holster that rides above and slightly behind the hip under the gun hand. You do not want a design that holds the gun in place with a safety strap, unless it can be released with a flick of the thumb as the hand closes over the pistol. After wearing a comfortable rig for a day or two, you will get quite accustomed to its presence.

Some jewelry and other retail stores in high-crime areas have armed their employees with revolvers carried in open sight, on the theory that the prospect of resistance will discourage would-be robbers.

Although such a show of force deters many criminals, it can be taken by some as a challenge: if your conspicuously-armed store is hit, your antagonists will be expecting to shoot, or worse, will walk in shooting. You and your people will probably be cut down before you can touch your holstered pistols. It is a bad idea to broadcast the fact that you have weapons. Remember that, in virtually any gunfight situation in the store, the odds are with the intruder, and surprise is one of the only two possible advantages you may have. The other is proficiency.

The ability to use your gun effectively is not only an asset, but indeed a responsibility. You must become sufficiently adept to be sure (a) that you will not endanger standers-by with wild shots, and (b) that you can neutralize an armed, violent offender before he terminates innocent lives. The handgun is the most difficult firearm to shoot accurately and rapidly; skill comes only with practice. Spend some time at a local gun club or police pistol range, learning the fundamentals of marksmanship and gun-handling from experts. Practice quick-draw, *but only with an unloaded weapon.*

Many of the guns now being kept in jewelry stores are not suitable for close-quarters use. Rifles and shotguns should not be considered for store defense weapons, because they are too long and bulky to conceal or quickly bring into action; moreover, the rifle's extreme power and the shotgun's spreading pattern of fire prohibit their use in a closed-in area that may contain innocent parties.

Two types of handguns are available, the revolver and the semi-automatic pistol. Due to basic differences in design, the double-action revolver is slightly bulkier, less likely to malfunction, easier to operate, and can be fired instantly without requiring a safety catch.

The automatic has greater cartridge capacity, is quicker to reload, and lends itself to accurate rapid fire. For safety's sake, however, most automatics demand that either a safety be released, or a cartridge pumped from the magazine into the firing chamber, before the gun can be used (an exception being the double-action automatics typified by the German Walther). It may be said that the automatic pistol is a bit easier to shoot accurately, while the revolver's simpler mechanism is easier and safer to operate. For this reason, the revolver is the best choice for the non-expert. Obsolete Western style single-action revolvers and derringer pistols have an unacceptably slow rate of fire.

High-powered guns—the .45 automatic or the .357, .41 and .44 Magnum revolvers—are too powerful to control without extensive training. The Magnum bullets, too, are likely to penetrate a criminal's body and go on to strike down bystanders, one reason they are not issued to urban police; the .38 Super Automatic, and the 9 m/m cartridge used in the popular Luger and Walther P-38, share this dangerously excessive penetrating power.

Conversely, .25 and .32 caliber guns are not potent enough to instantly neutralize a violent opponent, unless the bullets are placed with surgical precision. The only small-caliber handgun worth thinking about at all is a high quality .22 firing the long rifle hollowpoint cartridge, for two reasons: mild report and absence of recoil make it relatively easy for the novice to shoot with speed and accuracy, and the extremely low cost of ammunition encourages skill-building practice. There is an axiom to the effect that a hit with a .22 is preferable to a miss with a .45. Still, the .38 Special revolver or .380 automatic should be considered the best compromise of power and controllability.

The optimum gun is a double-action Colt or Smith & Wesson police-type service revolver. The medium-sized models designed for uniformed officers are best for storing in one place, but too large and heavy to conceal discreetly on the person; for the latter application the small-framed, 1½ lb. versions with "snub-nosed" barrels and rounded handles—the type used by most detectives and plainclothesmen—are much better.

It is most unlikely that your store defense gun will ever have to be used for its intended purpose. Yet if it should come to pass that, in your best judgment, there is no other choice, you should follow these rudiments of the ugly art and science of gunfighting:

If you anticipate an armed confrontation be certain to have your own gun in your hand before it begins; otherwise, remember that the odds are vastly against you. Try to get your opponent's eyes off you before you go for your gun, and remember that once you have made your move you are committed—if you hesitate at this point you will be shot, and with you perhaps every innocent party in the store. If time permits, take what cover you can.

Clear the gun with one swift, fluid motion, and fire as soon as the gun comes into line with your target. Holding the gun with both hands if possible, aim for a specific part of your opponent's body—preferably the chest, since the head is too small and bobbing a target except at point blank range—and keep firing until your opponent is unable to shoot back. Never aim to wound or disable.

If you are confronted with multiple opponents, try first to neutralize the most dangerous, that is, the one with the deadliest weapon or the one better able to shoot you in your present position. If you are wounded, your dominant thought must be to continue firing; if you fall, your enraged antagonists will almost certainly shoot you again where you lie.

When the encounter ends, ascertain that your opponent(s) can offer no further threat. Make sure there are no accomplices stationed outside. Do not approach them without assistance or with an empty gun. Even if they appear dead, they may be shamming. Clear all weapons out of their reach, including your own. If you have occasion to hold a disarmed criminal at gunpoint, keep him at least ten feet away spread-eagled on the floor, or with his hands high, or with elbows extended, fingertips touching the shoulders; shoot if he tries to move or close the distance.

Never pursue or fire after a fleeing thief, and avoid at all costs carrying a gun duel into the street. Call the police, without turning your back. If there are gunshot wounds to be treated, see to the nonbelligerents first, and use standard procedures for shock, hemorrhage, and resuscitation until emergency units arrive.

If the preceding suggestions sound harsh and repulsive, it is because they reflect the unpleasant nature of the subject. The uninitiated tend to make two kinds of mistakes with firearms: they either use guns when they shouldn't, or do not use them properly in the rare circumstances when they should.

The ultimate function of the gun you keep for defense is not warning or intimidation, but destruction, and if you cannot accept this you have no business with weapons, for the possession or display of one without the demonstrable intent to use it can precipitate a graver situation than that which it was intended to prevent.

Chapter 7
A Gun in your Home

There are probably more firearms kept as house defense weapons than for all other civilian security purposes combined. There are two distinct classes of home defense weapons: those that are kept strictly for that reason, and sporting firearms stored in such a manner as to be accessible in the event of an emergency. Counting this last category, probably half the homes in America, if not more, are armed against intruders. Those hunting and target guns aren't just thrown in to fatten the statistic of armed homes, either. "What would I do if someone broke in?" is a thought that has flashed across the mind of every man or woman who keeps a firearm, for whatever peaceful purpose—and, for that matter, most people who don't. Everyone who keeps guns has considered, however briefly, the possibility of an armed confrontation in the home. And herein lies the problem: the only thought most people have given to the use of a defense gun has been cursory at best. "Look at this!" they say indignantly over the morning paper, as they read of some atrocity committed on some innocent family by armed criminals who broke into their home. "By God, if anyone tried that here, I'd get my gun and . . . " This is usually the sum total of the pre-analysis most householders have given to the possibility of a shooting situation in the household.

The average American has more misconceptions about lethal force in the home than in any other self-defense situation. He not only has little understanding of his legal position under these circumstances; he has no idea of how to conduct himself if, by infinitesimal chance, the day comes when his home actually is turned into a battleground he must defend against armed criminals.

The Homeowner's Rights of Lethal Force

This factor is discussed in depth in a separate chapter. So are selection of weapons, and how to keep them safe yet ready in the family quarters. The main thing to remember at this point is the "home as castle" concept: the invaded householder may legally stand his ground instead of backing off. He has more latitude here than in any other self-defense situation. He is no longer a peaceful citizen but, in effect, a soldier with all the military edge of advance defensive planning and unannounced counter-assault.

The Householder's Disadvantage

There are few situations where you will be on even an equal footing with an armed intruder. Only if you become aware of his presence and lay a careful ambush before he realizes you are prepared, will you have an upper hand. In almost any intrusion situation, be it in the depths of the night or during waking hours, the intruder will have surprise in his favor, and this is an almost insurmountable advantage to him.

Relatively few such assaults occur in the daytime, though they seem to be increasing if newspaper reports are any indication. Almost invariably, the results are nightmarish, since criminals who are depraved enough or stoned enough to break into an occupied dwelling during the day are either bent on vicious attack, or volatile enough to respond with extreme savagery if their minds, out of touch with reality, take offense at the natural reactions of their terrified and outraged victims.

In daylight breaks, a common procedure is to knock on the door, and gain either complete entry or a foot in the threshhold on some pretext (salesman, stranded driver, accident victim, or whatever). This ploy has been used at night as well. Such an entrance is almost impossible to guard against; if a knock comes at the door at this moment, are you going to put down this book and fetch a gun before you answer it? (Well, maybe you might. There are areas in the United States where attacks have been so frequent that some householders keep guns within immediate reach at all times. One famous Washington, D.C. personage made news not long ago when he answered a late-night knock with a long-barrelled revolver in his hand.)

Where *do* you stand when an intruder, or a group of them, have entered your home and have you and the other occupants at weapon-point? The frightening answer is that you stand on the edge of death, with little but the intruder's whim to keep you on this side of the void. Cooperation is paramount, for a foolish attempt to disarm a gunman could provoke him or his band into committing a massacre.

52

Rape or similar outrages are statistically likely in such instances. Whether the prevention of rape is worth the risk of triggering a wholesale slaughter is not a choice anyone can make for you—or, indeed, one that any individual at the scene can make for the other innocent parties present. I do recall reading of one situation, the invasion of a dinner party by a group of armed men who forced sexual acts on some of the women present, that was later analyzed in depth by a newspaper publisher. Afer reviewing the statements given by the victims, it appeared that there were several moments when the invaders had their attention focused on the sexual assault, and had left themselves vulnerable if even one of the guests had been carrying a gun. Sadly, none were.

The only exception to the great likelihood of wanton violence is when a householder *enters unexpectedly* and catches a burglar in the act during the daytime. Many B & E men specialize in hitting suburban homes during the time when the dwellers are at work or school (or fetching the children home from school—2:30 to 3:00 p.m. is a peak hour for burglaries in many suburban communities). The average burglar is not so dangerous as a mugger or holdup man, but neither is he as timid a creature as some criminologists would have the public believe. Many do carry guns and knives, and almost all can be considered armed in light of the fact that the pry-bars and screwdrivers that comprise their burglar tools can double as lethal blunt or sharp instruments.

The psychology of the burglar is too complex to cram into a capsule statement. He recognizes the possibility of confrontation with a householder, and usually has decided beforehand that he won't permit himself to be captured. His reluctance to carry a gun stems less from his concern for his potential victim than from a fear of heavier penalties if caught. Still, he is not in the class with the stickup man, who makes a confrontation on every job, and must always be considered capable of killing if crossed. Finally, it must be remembered that a growing number of burglars are drug addicts, whose response to the householder's surprise entrance is dangerously unpredictable.

Night encounters are much more likely and, at least in relation to daytime assaults, sometimes more controllable. Still, the advantages are almost all with the intruder. Let us consider the classic case, the burglar who breaks in during the night while the family is asleep.

You, the head of the family, are awakened out of a sound slumber. It will be at least a few minutes, if you're an average man, before your reflexes and the acuteness of your sensory perception reach full capactiy.

You're eyes are adjusted to neither darkness nor light, and won't be for a matter of minutes. Your first reflex upon being alarmed into wakefulness, will be to turn on the lights. Even a 25-watt bulb on a night table lamp will cause your irises to contract; if you flick on a bright bedroom light or reading lamp, as you have probably found out already, the intense light will be so dazzling that you may experience an actual shock effect: your head snaps back involuntarily, your eyelids squinch shut forcibly, and your eyes hurt from the bright flash. Between the jarring transitionfrom dark to light, and the pressure in the eye sockets from squeezing the eyelids tightly shut, your eyes have been thrown momentarily out of focus. You may also experience floating patches of color that can obscure and distract your line of vision.

Altogether, you are not in ideal shape to be fighting for your or your family's lives.

These are the main factors, but there are others. One is that you are caught undressed, and even if it does occur to you to dress before investigating the disturbance, you probably won't have time if your household actually has been invaded by criminals. This is not as inconsequential as it may seem: whether or not clothes make the man, nakedness can certainly un-make him in a stressful confrontation with clothed opponents. A nude or pajama'd man is a vulnerable man, if only because he feels a sense of unpreparedness and awkwardness that can be fatal in a moment when he needs every ounce of confidence and decisiveness that he possesses. Always, if possible, put on at least your pants before making a confrontation. Shoes are optional: unless they're crepe-soled, they prevent your walking silently, yet shod feet can be precious weapons if it comes to a hand-to-hand struggle.

Your opponent, remember, is fully clothed and prepared, armed, and wider than wide awake—tension has dumped a load of adrenalin into his bloodstream that enhances his already sharp watchfulness to a superhuman degree. He is performing an act he has probably planned beforehand. He has long since decided how

Proper way for home defender to check for prowlers. Back to wall, he moves down edge of staircase to reduce stair squeak. Both flashlight and .45 are ready (however, finger should be off trigger).

he will respond to a householder's sudden presence, and is half-ready for it even if he doesn't hear you coming. His eyes are adjusted to the darkness.

He is better prepared than you are.

The best course of action is not to go and investigate, although you probably will anyway. It is obviously unfeasible to call the police—or to barricade yourself behind the bed for the duration of the night—every time you hear a squeak in the kitchen. But if there is a real reason to believe that someone has broken in, you would be foolish to walk out and confront him. Let us presume that you have no doubt that intruders are present, and consider the variables that will determine your response.

1) *Home layout.* Despite all that your opponents have going for them, you have one great advantage: you're on your own turf. You can probably find your way around your dwelling in the dark, if you've lived there any length of time. What you probably haven't noticed—and probably won't until some night when you're stalking from room to room in semi-darkness, half-waiting to be pounced on—is how many nooks and crannies there are to hide in. Just for the hell of it, spend an evening sometime playing hide and seek with your kids, in the house with the lights out. You'll be amazed at how many places they'll find to conceal themselves. And don't think a six-foot housebreaker can't squeeze himself into the hiding places your four-foot child finds.

If you fear that your home may one day become the arena for mortal combat between you and one or more intruders, scrutinize it *now* with the eye of a general selecting a battleground. Let's say, for instance, that your kitchen opens into your dining room. If the kitchen is lit up, but the dining room isn't, what areas of the latter will be illuminated by the light that spills in from the kitchen? Which parts will be in deep shadow? How about if the light is shining in from the hall?

Lighting is of paramount importance in any after-dark gunfight situation. You must know where an opponent can be waiting in ambush when you come downstairs to investigate, or where you yourself may take cover if you see an intruder before he sees you. In half or three-quarters of an hour, you can go through your dwelling, checking out each room and hall with different lighting combinations.

Try to avoid positions where you are plainly visible to one who may be watching from an unlighted area. If, for instance, you are making a confrontation across a staircase, you will probably command a light switch at the head of the stairs. Switch on the downstairs lights while keeping your own level in darkness. Some people would try the opposite, on the old "High Noon" concept: "Keep the sun behind you, partner, to blind the gunman facing you."

Bull. The illumination from a conventional hall light is not sufficiently bright or focused to blind a man some forty or fifty feet away. It will, however, do a great job of setting you up like a target in a shooting gallery.

2) *Control of the sleeping area.* Your response to an illegal entry must be predicated on one basic architectural factor: whether your living area (not counting basement or attic) is contained in one floor or two. The man in a two-story home has a huge advantage: since the illegal entry will usually take place on the first floor, he has the option of "localizing the action" downstairs if he wakes up in time. Presumably, all sleeping quarters are on the second floor. The family is therefore close enough together to be successfully protected from the invaders below.

Your first act, having armed yourself, should be to ascertain that the person downstairs is not a member or guest of the family. It is entirely possible that someone has gone downstairs for a midnight snack, or maybe your teenage son, whom you didn't wait up for, brought home an intoxicated buddy to sleep it off on the living room sofa. Some hideous tragedies have occurred this way; not as many as implied by Carl Bakal and others who advocate disarming the public, but enough to teach a lesson of caution.

To make sure that all in the household are on the second floor, you have a choice of calling out to them, or padding softly to each bedroom to awaken them one by one. The second approach has two advantages: the intruders will not be warned that you are aware of their presence, and you eliminate the possibility of a half-asleep child walking out, perhaps into the line of fire, to see what the shouting is all about.

It may be a good idea to have key or sturdy dead-bolt locks on the doors of the master bedroom, and of the quarters of those children mature enough not to lock themselves behind it after a family argument or whatever. The doors shouldn't be *kept* locked, necessarily—that sort of thing makes for a rotten family atmosphere—but it's nice to know that in an emergency your family can be safely barricaded for at least a minute or two before the lock gives way.

If you have reason to believe that there are armed men on the floor beneath you, have your family stay on their beds if they can. If alarmed, the burglars may fire through the ceiling at the sound of your voice or footsteps, and a high-powered bullet, if it misses a cross-beam, can often penetrate the second floor. In this event, the mattress offers some degree of protection.

3) *Control of the confrontation scene.* At this point, hopefully, you have determined that your people are all on the second floor, and that the intruders are confined to the first. Since you probably won't be foolish enough to go down to attempt a citizen's arrest, your first concern should be that you control all points of entry to the second floor. In most homes, this will be a single stairway; if you have two stairways to watch, summon and arm your wife or eldest child to cover the one the intruders are least likely to use.

Call the police. Every home should have an extension telephone on the night table in the master bedroom. It's cheap insurance against all kinds of sudden household emergencies when seconds may count in calling for help.

Control the lights in the hall, and especially the stairs. There should be a master light switch outside (or, if you want to pay for rewiring, inside) your main bedroom.

Remember that the staircase will be the principal confrontation area; under no circumstances should you permit an intruder to reach the second floor. If the intruder is approaching the stairs, you can either shout a warning or ambush him as he comes into your line of fire.

At this point, I do not favor a verbal warning. In deliberately entering the occupied home, the intruder has indicated that he plans to deal violently with the occupants; if he does not realize that the occupants are home, he is so stoned or otherwise unbalanced that he cannot be expected to respond in a normal fashion to your challenge. Whether homicidal or unbalanced, he has proven himself to be incapable of being reasoned with. To challenge him at this point is only to make him aware of your presence, and thus mitigate your advantage.

If he is facing you *with a weapon visible*, neutralize him in-

58

stantly. If you come upon him from behind, of course, you have the option of giving a challenge, so long as you understand that you jeopardize your own position by so doing. But what if you yell "Hold it," or "Drop your gun," and the tense housebreaker reflexively spins around toward you, gun in hand? At this point, you will have to shoot anyway. Even if you do, you have greatly increased your own chances of taking a knife or bullet. If you hesitate when he turns, he will very likely kill you the instant he sees you, especially if he sees that you are armed and hesitant to pull your trigger.

Remember: once you have ascertained that you are dealing with hostile intruders, the staircase becomes a free-fire zone.

If you live in a single-story home, any intrusion situation will put you on the same footing as the man in a two-story dwelling who is confronted with intruders on the second floor. *You do not usually have the practical option of calling out a challenge when you and the armed intruder are in sight of each other, even if his back is turned.*

The preceding may sound brutal. It is, necessary. The call of the challenge before the draw is a myth based on an Old West code that never existed in real life. Adherence to this precept of fair play has cost the lives of many police officers and law abiding citizens, who perhaps never realized that their antagonists did not follow the code.

The average American has never witnessed—probably never even read a complete, official report of—a real, armed confrontation. But he has seen hundreds on the screen. On TV, the one who has the drop on his opponent yells "Hold it right there," and the gunman freezes, then slowly opens his hand to let his weapon fall. But in real life, the criminal does not freeze at the unexpected challenge.

He turns. Swiftly and suddenly, he snaps around toward the alarming voice. He turns instinctively with the weapon in his hand, his tense, adrenalin-filled body exploding into reflexive response. If he does not pull the trigger automatically as he faces you, it will be the first response that occurs to his hair-trigger nervous system when he sees you.

You, on the other hand, are jarred by his unexpected reaction. Startled, you hesitate, thrown off your planned course of action. At the instant when you stand between surprise and response, his surprise has already *resolved* into response.

And he pulls the trigger first.

If you have ascertained that the man you have the drop on is a deliberate intruder into your occupied home (and therefore, by definition, a deranged or vicious enemy); if you are certain that he has a weapon in or at hand; if you and he are in positions where he can shoot or stab you—

Shoot him. In the back, if you have to. And keep shooting him until he is unable to shoot back.

Yes, he might have frozen at the command. He might have dropped his weapon, and allowed you to hold him for the police.

His response is as instinctive as yours would be in his place, and whether he turns as a natural reaction to a sudden loud noise with a weapon that just happens to be in his hand, or whether he is reacting to any challenge which he has prepared himself beforehand to kill in answer to, you don't know. You probably never will. The point is that you can't afford to find out, because there's a good chance that his reaction is the last thing that will register in your mind before he kills you. It's possible that murder wasn't his intention when he turned toward you with weapon in hand, and it's a thought that will stay with you for the rest of your life if you kill him. But he called it, not you. If it ever happens, remember that it was he who set the stage, he who offered you the choice you didn't want and couldn't afford to make in his favor.

If you analyze a number of official police reports of confrontations with armed criminals, you will reach the inescapable conclusion that sudden and violent resistance is, statistically, a much more likely response than surrender. And if the intruder's armed response is successful, if he neutralizes you, it is entirely possible that he will massacre the household, whether to eliminate witnesses to the murder he has committed, or in an insane orgy of killing triggered by the mortal combat you let him win by handing him the advantage you had held moments before.

Investigating "The noise in the kitchen"

If you called the police every time you heard a squeak in the kitchen, it wouldn't be long before the boys in the station put you on the crank list. A call to the police is the first priority when you have real reason to believe you've been broken into. But there are times when you'll want to investigate a suspicious noise just to put your or your wife's mind at ease.

Before you do, turn on the bedroom lights, as low as possible, and wait a few minutes. This will give you more opportunity to check out the situation with your ears, and will permit your eyes to focus and adjust to moderate-to-dim light.

Dress before you leave the bedroom. Remember to put on your glasses if you normally wear them. Have your wife at the phone if possible, standing by for an emergency call if she hears sounds of a scuffle. Have her dial the first digits of the police station number beforehand, so she can dial the last digit for an immediate connection. This may not always work, depending on the vagaries of your local phone system. Give it a practice run beforehand, with a 15 or 20-minute interval between the last two digits. If she hears sounds of a struggle or confrontation, she should have been instructed in advance to give the address, tell the desk sergeant that a violent armed break is in progress, request an ambulance, and repeat the address. Her role in assisting you further will be considered in the chapter on "Women and Defense Guns."

Take a flashlight with you. I like a multi-celled, heavy-barrelled flash because it penetrates shadows better, and doubles as a last-resort nightstick. If you know someone who sells police equipment, pay $15-30 for a Kel-light or Tru-Grit police flashlight with a potent beam and a heavy body suitable for hand-to-hand combat.

When you leave the bedroom, move out quickly into the outside area, a few steps beyond the door in case a stealthy burglar is waiting outside the bedroom.

Hold your loaded gun firmly, with your finger *outside* the trigger guard until you actually see or hear an intruder. A single-action automatic pistol should be cocked and locked with the thumb on the release catch. Hold the handgun at your beltline, your wrist locked against your hip; don't hold it out in front of you, because an intruder may be around a corner waiting to bring a tire iron down across your extended wrist.

The possibility of such a lurking intruder suggests that you walk in the center of a room or hall, so that he will have to move far enough out from his place of concealment to give you at least a moment of warning. On the other hand, walking through the center of a room will often make you a better target by silhouetting you in the light from the room behind. Only by familiarizing yourself in this regard with each room in your own home, can you determine the best course of approach to each.

When moving over a staircase, you should walk as a burglar walks—along the edge of the stairs, against the wall, if one is there. The steps are most strongly supported at this point, and less likely to creak. Use this same technique when moving down halls: if you hug the wall, the support of the floor beams there will keep the floorboards from squeaking under your weight.

Take these advantages. You'll need all of them, and more. The law-abiding householder is at a great situational, physical, and psychological disadvantage against a criminal who breaks into his home. He will need all the instruction given in this chapter, plus a portion of luck and a degree of marksmanship skill, if he is to successfully protect himself and his family in the unlikely event that criminals should break in to threaten their lives.

Two final cautions, to prevent your being shot by a policeman instead of a burglar. First, having called the police, *stay where you are*. The police team that answers the burglary call will be walking into a tense situation with guns drawn; it would be most unwise to meet them with a gun in your own hand. Finally, if you and they are both stalking through the dark rooms, it's a good bet they'll see you first: they're trained to spot people in the dark. When they see you, they'll probably challenge, and you'll probably turn suddenly toward the sound, like the burglar discussed previously. If you do, you will quite probably be shot where you stand. Depending on how urgent the call was, they may break in themselves through door or window. The nearest unit responding may contain plainclothes officers, or, in small communities, the call may bring an off-duty cop who didn't have time to don a uniform. A casually dressed man with a .38 in his hand will look a lot like the burglar you came downstairs expecting to find.

By not staying out of the way after making the call, you have set the stage for an accidental shooting on either side. A court could deem it contributory negligence.

The second warning is one applicable to virtually *all* armed confrontations a civilian may be involved in: *never* pursue a fleeing suspect once he has ceased to be a danger to you. Unless he is a maniac who has just wiped out half your family, you need feel no compulsion to chase him down and capture him (and even in that event, you will probably accomplish more if you stay behind to call in aid for the wounded).

Citizens arrest, and procedures for holding a suspect who has surrendered, will be discussed in separate chapters. So will the extent of the homeowner's liability for wounds suffered by criminals or bystanders.

Chapter 8
A Gun in the Street

Civilians who buy guns for street defense tend to think that their very possession will alleviate the dangers that made them get a gun in the first place. For instance, one who is normally afraid to walk through a certain area may, after he buys a gun and acquires a carry permit, go back to walking through that area. After all, he reasons, isn't it safe for him to go where he pleases now that he packs a gun?

No, it isn't. In fact, a civilian who wears a sidearm should be even more careful to avoid situations dangerous enough that it might later appear that he was looking for trouble. True, you may now feel safe strolling through Central Park at 3:00 a.m. But a prosecutor in a self-defense shooting case will ask, "But what were you doing there at that ungodly hour? Were you *looking* for a legal excuse to shoot somebody?"

If accosted on the street, you should not go for your gun immediately unless you are directly, physically attacked (as, for instance, in a mugging or rape attempt). If confronted by a bunch of show-off punks who just want to throw their weight around, don't throw yours back. Humor them, if need be. Take all the verbal abuse they give you, and don't take up the challenge. Some will say that submissiveness encourages wise punks to escalate their threats, the way the smell of fear drives vicious animals to attack. Maybe so, but a show of resistance will usually put the wise-asses in a position where they may feel compelled to assert themselves physically to prove themselves.

In anticipation of such an incident, I carry a five-dollar bill wrapped around a match book when I'm walking in a high-crime area. If I encounter a bunch of punks I can't avoid by crossing the street, and if they give me a lot of jive, I'll toss the fiver to the ringleader (the matchbook gives enough weight so I can toss it to someone who's still several feet away from me). I'll tell him I don't want any trouble, and suggest that he buy the boys a round of beers on me.

Maybe it won't work. Maybe it'll just whet his appetite to go for my wallet. I'm betting that it will satisfy the ego need that drove him to confront me. You may think it's a chickenshit approach. Maybe it is. I only know that it's easily worth five or ten bucks to me not to have to shoot somebody.

Of course, the above is relative only to punks who block your way on the street and shoot their mouths off. In an actual assault situation, you are obviously under no moral or practical obligation to "buy off" your assailants.

But you should still follow a pattern of escalation, if you see the attack coming in time. Try to get out of the way, first. If you can't, draw your gun. If there's time and if they're unarmed, give a verbal warning: "Stay back or I'll shoot." If they keep coming at you, a warning shot may be in order, though I don't usually recommend it for civilians. The sight of a gun should be warning enough.

If they ignore your warnings, still keep coming, and are close enough to be capable of inflicting death or grave bodily harm upon you or your companions, you are justified in shooting them.

All street situations don't occur slowly enough to go through that sequence of escalation. The last time I was jumped in a parking lot, the only warning I had was that I noticed one of my assailants standing around trying to look inconspicuous (the other was crouching behind a car, waiting to pounce). When I first became suspicious, I opened my coat so I could better reach the straight-draw holster (I'd have been better off with the gun in my coat pocket). When they came at me I drew my gun. They stopped in their tracks, and stayed there, with their hands where I could see them. I put the .38 snubnose in my overcoat pocket, my hand still around it, and kept going, watching them as I left. Not a word had been spoken.

No, I didn't call the police. The thugs would have been long gone by the time the cops got there. No, I didn't make a citizen's arrest. I wasn't carrying handcuffs, and they might have jumped me as I marched them back to the motor inn I had just left. Besides, I had no concrete proof that they had jumped me. It would have been my word against theirs. They could have said I was a nut who had pulled a gun on them.

It has occurred to me since that the pair might have attacked other people after that night. They would have anyway if I'd reported them, after they were inevitably released for lack of evidence. I prefer to think that my armed response scared the shit out of them, and made them give up the practice of assaulting people in parking lots. But I'm probably kidding myself.

Obviously, if you are attacked directly by a mugger, rapist, or robber, you have the right to shoot. But be governed by practical considerations, i.e., don't draw on a drawn gun. A definite danger is that your assailants will hold you at gunpoint, shake you down, and take your gun. It's a good reason for keeping a .38 in your coat pocket, in your hand, when walking through high-crime areas.

Chapter 9
A Gun in your Car

The carrying of a special "car gun," or the constant keeping of a gun in the car, is a more common practice than it probably should be.

The relative laws with regard to carrying guns in automobiles are listed in the gun law compendium elsewhere in this book. Essential self-defense rulings—for instance, the requirement of retreat when assaulted on a public highway where you have a legitimate right to be—apply equally no matter where you are. One exception: your picking up a hitchhiker in a community or state where the practice is forbidden, might compromise your innocence and thus your "perfect" right of self-defense if he later attacks you and you have to shoot him.

Only practical circumstances change in a self-defense situation that takes place on a public road. Obviously, the picking up of transients is a no-no. To most of us, avoidance of hitchhikers is like the wearing of seat belts and rubbers: one of those things *Readers's Digest* and Mother says is good for us, that we don't take too seriously.

Be honest. Would you or would you not pick up a hitchhiker, even a rather scruffy one, in the middle of a downpour or a Northeaster? Most everybody else would, too. But a depraved criminal is no less dangerous for being soaked to the skin. Maybe he's even meaner for being left in the rain by the motorists who came before you, and is looking for someone to take it out on.

If you must be a Good Samaritan, at least give yourself and your legitimate passengers a chance. *Never* pick up hitchhikers when you have women or children in the car—you expose them to an unnecessary danger, and their presence will hamper your practical self-defense if, indeed, your worst fears are realized. *Never* pick up more than one hitchhiker at a time, and *never* allow one in the back seat.

When a hitchhiker first approaches your car, he should find the doors locked and windows shut. If his intentions are criminal, he may tip his hand—by drawing a knife as he runs up, for instance.

Another warning sign is if he jerks violently at the door, what the statutes call "violent and tumultuous entry" when speaking of housebreaks; he may have been poised to pounce on you as soon as he entered the car.

What if he shows a gun? Watch him in the rear-view mirror as he approaches. If he is keeping one hand out of sight, drive away forthwith. If he confronts you at the door with a drawn gun, you are in a rotten position. You'll probably be fired upon as you draw, and you can't drive away fast enough: the lag between the thrust of your right leg and the response of acceleration is long enough for him to shoot you before the car even moves. There's no real solution. Kind of makes you wish you didn't pick up hitch-hikers, huh?

Obviously, you can't already have a gun drawn on every hitch-hiker you pick up—it sort of defeats your purpose in stopping. Besides, suppose your newfound passenger notices the gun, and considers it strange enough a thing to report it to police ("I was just picked up by a guy who pointed a gun at me as I got into the car").

Be especially leery of picking up girls. A new kind of instant blackmail had evolved from the practice of hitchhiking: a young girl, once in the car, will give you a choice between $20.00 or a report to the police that you tried to molest her. This does not concern us directly here, but consider a related possibility, an actual attempt by the girl at armed assault.

Before you use your gun, consider the newspaper headlines tomorrow morning: LOCAL MAN PICKS UP, SLAYS TEEN GIRL. Better you should avoid entirely a situation that could place you in a perilous situation from which you dare not extricate yourself with the full force at your command, for fear of moral error or public criticism. This is one of the few principles we have learned from the epoch of Vietnam. It applies as well to individuals as to countries.

Car Guns

I do not favor the selection of particular guns for auto defense alone. Almost all such guns are selected for their ability to penetrate auto bodies—9 m/m's, heavy Magnums, and similar weapons.

Actually, it is most unlikely that you will ever be involved in a situation where you will have to shoot through an automobile. Even for highway cops, it's a rare occurrence. Few State Patrols and other rural police even bother to keep metal piercing ammo in the cruisers for their own .38's and .357's, which are almost invariably loaded with soft-nosed anti-personnel ammo. That is because these officers realize that gunfights encountered in the course of their highway duties are likely to involve point-blank, rather than high-speed running, confrontations. Cops, who have to pursue and capture fleeing criminals, seldom have to shoot at cars. It would be hard to think of a situation where the civilian *ever* would.

The ideal gun? Whatever you normally carry for personal defense. One caution: the blast of a high-powered handgun in the tiny enclosed space of a car with rolled up windows, is literally deafening. The concussion can cause permanent ear damage. Be sure you *have* to shoot before you risk forfeiting your sense of hearing as well as the life of a rambunctious hitchhiker.

Where Should It Be Kept?

It is never a good idea to keep a gun stored in a car, for two reasons. First, the only place where you can get to it before an unauthorized occupant does is between the seat and the left front door, say in a map pocket. Under the seat, or between the seat cushions, the gun will soon fill with gritty dirt and become useless.

The second point is that a gun in a car is constantly left unattended and vulnerable to theft.

Finally, the purpose of having a gun at all is to protect *you*, and since a defensive situation is much more likely to crop up while you're out of the car, a gun in the glove compartment is of limited defensive use.

Blockades

If you are in a blockade situation—people or cars are arrayed across the road, forcing you to stop—you are in a kind of danger that is becoming more and more frequent. In certain inner city areas, it is not uncommon for gangs of youths to approach cars at stop lights and demand monetary tribute on threat of having windows smashed in. In certain areas of New York City, for example, motorists keep their doors locked and windows up for fear of being dragged out of their cars.

Nor are the hinterlands free from such threats. The Kangamangus Highway in New Hampshire's White Mountains was at one time infested with hippies who would set up roadblocks, and extort a few dollars protection money from motorists who didn't want their cars smashed. They would set up at a remote point where they would have time to terrorize several carloads of tourists before the first victim could get to a telephone; they'd be gone long before the police arrived. Legend has it that the practice ceased after a group of Green Berets on maneuvers in the White Mountains spent a few weekends cruising the Kangamangus in civvies, beating up marauders caught in the act.

Not long ago, a young Vermonter was forcibly stopped at an impromptu roadblock set up by a local gang of motorcycle bums called "The Mind Benders." The man showed them his gun, and was allowed to pass. He was arrested for the act, and convicted and nominally sentenced for disorderly conduct.

What to do in an illegal roadblock situation? A prudent man will take one of two alternatives: make a U-turn and split, or cough up the money. It rankles the spirit, but it's a lot cheaper than court costs, or antagonizing the gang into an attack with your family in the car.

When you have to use the threat of a gun, be discreet. Don't brandish it flamboyantly. In most cases, your potential assailant will be close enough to the car that, being upright, he can look down into the passenger compartment and see your low-held weapon. Never try to shoot from a moving car, especially with your left hand if you're not a southpaw. The shot will almost certainly go wild, and if it strikes an innocent bystander, you will probably be considered negligent for firing from a speeding car.

If criminals are swarming over your car, trying to smash in windows or rip open doors, you have a better weapon than your gun. You are controlling a two-ton bludgeon. Put your car in gear, shout a warning, beep the horn, and drive. Start slowly unless the rocks are already flying through the windows. If that is the case, move. Don't try to deliberately run anyone down, that is, don't swerve out of your way to put the wheels to your assailants. Avoid them if you can, but not to the extent of going into a ditch and preventing your escape.

If a rock-throwing attacker is deliberately blocking your path, and you have no alternative route of escape, and if it really appears that a savage attack is about to begin or is already underway—go over the man in front of you. It can honestly be stated that you were making every reasonable effort in good faith, to avoid a situation that would have required the lethal force of your gun. Since you didn't deliberately run down the assailant in front of you, the act may or may not be considered lethal force. A device not built to be a deadly weapon becomes so only when used with intent to kill or injure. That's why it's important to make it obvious that, far from deliberately killing the man in front of you, you're making every effort to avoid harming anyone as you escape. This will be especially important if the court decides that the rocks or whatever did not constitute deadly weapons in the hands of your attackers.

There are not enough court precedents to make a definite statement either way. Apparently, while many such episodes have occurred, few have been processed through the justice machine.

Chapter 10
Deterrent Effect of Defense Handguns

I have often said that in a situation where the law-abiding citizen is criminally threatened with physical harm, the great saving force of the self-defense handgun will be demonstrated more in its psychological deterrent power than in its ballistic stopping power.

I don't deny the fact that there will be terrible moments where the intended victim will have no choice but to pull the trigger. But if the timing is right, and if the assailants are of the typical mettle of a mugger who wants an easy score and doesn't want to shed any of his own red blood to line his pockets with someone else's green money, the sight of your blue steel may be enough to turn some faces white and some spines yellow, and let you go on living your life uninterrupted in its own placid colors.

For instance, it is a cold February night. I am leaving a Holiday Inn located on the outskirts of what is listed in the FBI reports as one of the most crime-free cities in America. It is cold, bitter cold, with a savage Nor-Easter blowing. I button my topcoat over my suitjacket as I walk through the darkened parking lot to the very edge, where I had to leave my car. Alone in the car-filled lot is a young man in a thin pea-jacket, smoking a cigarette, lounging against the hood of a sedan.

On this night, in this weather, it is not a place to relax for a smoke. I look around the lot, wondering whom he is waiting for. There is no one to be seen.

I glance back at the young man, and he is already looking at me, and our eyes meet. I nod to him, the instinctive gesture of one human being meeting another in a lonely place. He turns sharply away, looking fixedly at nothing, and draws on his cigarette.

Alarm bells ring in my subconscious. Something is wrong here. The same instinct makes my right hand unbutton my topcoat and my suitcoat, to give that hand access to the Smith & Wesson

Chief's Special in its speed rig on my right hip. I feel the frigid wind knife through my chest. *You schmuck.* I think to myself, *if you get pneumonia and die, they'll list your cause of death as paranoia.* I keep walking. The young man, directly in my path, keeps looking away.

I pass within a few yards. And, suddenly, he moves.

The half-smoked cigarette (I remember it had a brown filter) is thrown to the ground, and with a violent sweep of his arm ("Marines, let's go!") he gestures toward a car in the parking lane behind him. And now a lupine face rises from behind a fender, its eyes on mine as the young man's are now, narrowed and hungry.

And they lunge. For me.

I am two people. One of me watches in fascination, never before having seen a human face in a frenzy that would draw the lips so far back from the teeth that the gums are showing. The other of me, without really thinking about it, draws the .38.

And, *voila*, another revelation. Never before, except in cartoons, have I seen people come skidding to a halt on the heels of their shoes, with their toes pointed skyward and their hands flailing for balance.

We stand looking at each other for a long moment. They can't see the wicked tips of the hollowpoint handloads in the chambers, and wouldn't recognize them if they did, because this is before the day when ACLU bleated to the world about Super Vel and police brutality. The gun isn't even pointed at them, just held casually at a 45° angle. But they know what it is, and they look at me with surprise. "No *fair*," they seem to be thinking. "*You're* not supposed to pull steel!"

I give them a big grin, partly because I often respond to stress situations with a touch of hysterical laughter, and partly because I can't think of anything relevant to say.

Then, I walk to my car, backwards, watching them with an occasional glance over each shoulder for a third mugger, who either isn't there or knows enough not to jump on someone with a piece.

And then I get in my car and drive away.

It has been a long time since that happened to me. I often wondered if I was wrong in not trying the citizen's arrest number (I didn't become a cop until later). I wondered if I left them out there to pounce somebody else.

But I knew *then* that it was their two words against my one, and

The deterrent effect of merely showing the weapon (along with clear intent to use it if necessary) quite often is sufficient to terminate a danger situation without bloodshed.

while *I* knew they hadn't come up to me to bum a cigarette, it might have been hard to convince a judge of that in a town where there supposedly isn't any street crime. I'd rather think that I scared enough out of them and they gave up trying to mug straight strangers who just might be "walking heavy."

Not long after that, I was in a major metropolis that doesn't try to hide its street crime problem because it can't. In broad daylight, I was accosted by a man-woman mugger team. The woman's deliberate staggering into me was supposed to throw me off balance and into the arms of her male friend. But I had worked with enough good judo teachers to stay on my feet, turn, and wind up facing her boyfriend with her on the other side.

He didn't brandish his knife like in "Blackboard Jungle" or "West Side Story." He just drew it. It was a fixed blade, a kitchen knife I think.

Matter-of-factly, with a big grin, he showed it to me.

Matter-of-factly, with a big grin, I showed him a four-inch .38 revolver.

Rather urgently, he shoved the bare knife back into his belt, and I hope he slashed himself. He raised his hands in a conciliatory gesture ("Don't shoot, we're all friends here, heh heh . . .") and waved the woman behind him to cross the street as he back pedalled himself. He stopped grinning, turned to her with his eyes widening now, and made a desperate "get the hell out of here" gesture. Then he looked back at me and grinned even wider as he continued his backward movement.

I grinned back and put the gun inside my sportshirt again. He turned and fled.

I did not try to apprehend him. I wasn't a cop then, either. And that city didn't give gun permits to out-of-state travellers, or, for that matter, to its own crime-plagued citizens. *He* would have gotten a free lawyer. *I* would have spent some time in their local clink and would still have a felony bust on my record. If I hadn't had the gun, he probably would still have gotten off with his free lawyer, and I would have wound up in the hospital and would still have the scars. Or maybe the worms would have eaten the scar tissue by now. Either way, it was easier to walk away whole with no blood on my hands. And none of mine on anyone else's.

It was some years later, and this time, I was wearing a police uniform. The call came over the radio and I hit the lights and siren. A drug-crazed suspect had forced his way into a suburban home on the edge of the community I patrolled.

He was gone when we got there, but he had already left a residue of fear that would never go away. He'd had the wife down on her living room couch when the husband, hearing her screams, grabbed his Walther .32 auto from his night-table drawer and ran to her aid.

The guy heard him coming, and threw himself to his feet to take the husband. The guy was big. Then he saw the pistol . . . and got small.

He backed out the door screaming threats, covering his face like a vampire in a late-show movie cringing from a crucifix. By the time the husband had chased him out, his wife had run to the bedroom closet and fetched the loaded 12-gauge. As the druggie stood on the lawn screaming obscene threats at the homeowner, the latter fired a round of birdshot into the air, and the attacker fled into the woods.

During the hours that followed, as I and a contingent of brother officers stalked the suspect through the woods, I reflected on the value of that little .32 automatic in that man's night-table drawer. We'd had a decent response time—we were on the scene less than a minute after getting the hysterical phone call—but as I crept through the pitch-black woods that night, listening to the sound of the bloodhounds, I couldn't help but wonder what might have happened if he *hadn't* had that little gun. I admit, I didn't reflect on it *too* much at the time, because I was more preoccupied with the sounds and movements around me as I still-hunted the brush with a Kel-Lite flashlight going on-and-off in one hand, and a Colt .45 automatic in the other. But I knew damn well that without the little .32, we might not have gotten the call until it was too late.

Later that night, when the thing was (bloodlessly) ended, that man came up to me and said, "Officer, my wife is afraid they're going to arrest me for threatening him with a gun. They aren't, are they?"

That gave me something to reflect on, too. I remembered those incidents back before I started wearing a badge, and how my first thought was that "they" could arrest me for defending myself against violent assault. At that moment, I was glad I'd taken the call as R/O (responding officer or reporting officer).

I put my hand on the guy's shoulder. I told him he wouldn't be arrested. I told him to come in to the police station Monday morning and see about getting a "carry" pistol permit. And then I gave him the address of a friend of mine who runs a police equipment shop, and promised him a discount on something bigger than a .32 automatic. Somewhere in between came a lecture on trusting the frail hook-and-eye lock on his screen door.

Wanna few more? I've got files full, and thank God, only a few of 'em happened to me. But the documentation is there, with me and a lot of other people, most of 'em cops: when an innocent person is menaced by a violent criminal who doesn't give a damn for any life but his own, the very presence of a firearm is often enough to turn the situation around, to make the attacker say, "Whoa! I didn't bargain for jeopardizing *my* life instead of *yours!*"

I reiterate: the very presence of a citizen's gun, as they rightfully say in the Armed Citizen column in AMERICAN-RIFLEMAN, often prevents bloodshed on either side. You'd think the ACLU and similar groups would appreciate that more than they do.

Despite all the junk "rape defense manuals" and similar pop lit, there's only one way you can talk a violent criminal out of harming you once he's picked you for a victim. What you have to do, is hit him with a deep, existential question, something that will make him re-examine and re-evaluate his own personal values and life style, his own hopes and dreams, as related to the moment at hand. It can even be phrased without words.

A question like, "You don't want me to have to shoot you in the face with this .38 Special, do you, scumbag?"

Chapter 11
Common Sense About Carrying Guns

The right of all law-abiding citizens to bear arms is beyond Constitutional doubt, though fine points of the Second Amendment remain the subject for heated debate. But beyond the general possession of firearms, the license to carry concealed, deadly weapons in public is not a right but a privilege. To be worthy of this privilege, one must be both discreet and competent with the weapon. The gun-carrying man who lacks either attribute is a walking time bomb.

Discretion

The man who wears a gun carries with it the power of life and death, and therefore the responsibility to deport himself with greater calm and wisdom than his unarmed counterpart, whose panic or misjudgment in crisis situations will have less serious consequences. The power of the gun is never ignored, no matter how accustomed one becomes to the weight on his hip. A man carrying a gun for the first time is acutely, even uncomfortably aware of its presence. After a time, he ceases to notice both the weight and the responsibility, not because he has forgotten them, but because they have both been assimilated into his bearing and demeanor.

Those who would ban the civilian ownership of defense guns feel that this absorption of potentially deadly power can create dangerous change in the character of the armed man. They fear that a man who before avoided quarrels, whether from reasonable or cowardly fear, will now be so fortified by the artificial potency of the gun that he will pick up on the slightest insult, perhaps escalating minor, everyday arguments into deadly confrontations.

Over many years of carrying guns, and of living in a part of the United States where the practice is commonplace among law-abiding citizens of all levels of society, I have learned otherwise.

In a normal, conscientious person, the presence of that deadly power engenders not belligerence, but an enhanced degree of self-control and coolness in tense moments of real or potential conflict. There are, I think, two reasons.

"If I hadn't been carrying a gun, I would have punched that wise-ass in the mouth." I have heard this sentiment many times. I have uttered it myself.

The responsible man who carries a legal gun does not respond to emotional provocation as he might if unarmed. An insult to one's wife by a punk on the street is a case in point. The instinctive reaction is a threat or a blow. The presence of a gun does not give a reasonable man unnatural arrogance in this situation; rather, it creates a restraint. He knows that what would otherwise be a fistfight could escalate at the moment he, an armed man, engaged the provocator in physical combat, and he knows that the responsibility for the outcome would be his. It forces him to respond to the dictates of reason, not those of outraged pride.

Secondly, the possession of the ultimate degree in personal, physical power gives him an edge that improves his footing in more ways than one. An unarmed man threatened with physical assault responds largely from fear. A danger he is ill prepared to cope with has two results: it clouds his thinking with fear, even panic, and it provokes him to extremes to ensure his own survival. For instance, the two responses may combine, inducing him to attack before the use of force has become entirely necessary.

He who is armed is not above fear, but he experiences it to a lesser degree. The knowledge that he is prepared to cope with and survive the worst, relieves his mind of the heaviest fear, and lets him turn his full mental powers toward a non-violent escape from the situation.

He can afford to try to talk or walk his way out of it. He's not giving up anything by holding off—his gun, and hopefully his skill with it, will still be the deciding factors if the assailants choose to make it a life or death situation. Another advantage is that he is under no social pressure to reinforce his masculinity with a counterattack: his possession of the gun, and the responsibility that accompanies it, give him an acceptable reason to excuse himself from the conflict.

There is another element of discretion to be considered when we discuss lawfully concealed guns. Even an ordinary man may

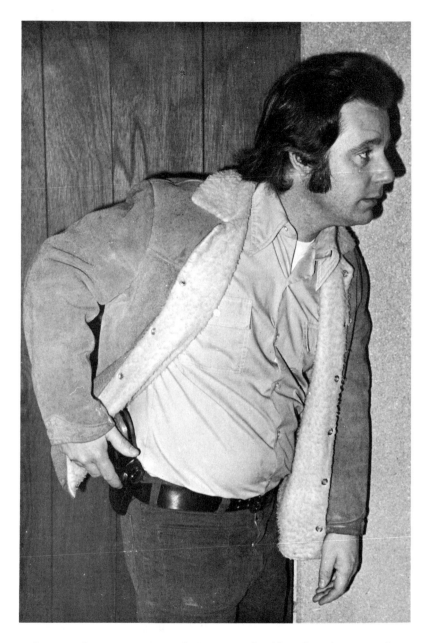

The man who carries a concealed weapon should not let it be seen unless he is about to use it.

feel an occasional perverse twinge of exhibitionism when he is wearing a firearm. In a society whose all-pervasive entertainment media have glorified men who carry guns, the possession of one can impart a glamorous—certainly a dramatic—image to the wearer. It can be tempting to reveal the fact that you're "carrying."

It is a temptation to be avoided. It serves no purpose; indeed, in our society, it can detract from your public image.

There is nothing inherently wrong with a civilian carrying a gun. I know bankers, attorneys, businessmen, reporters, and clergymen who consider a sidearm as much a part of their daily apparel as their wallet. But to non-gun-owners, it seems a somehow unwholesome practice, associated with criminals and paranoiacs. To them, a man who carries a gun for no immediate reason is . . . strange. They regard such a person as they would one who talked to himself.

We live according to social values that sometimes seem hard to fathom. While it is fashionable to champion certain rights of the individual—to privacy, to sexual preference, to the benefit of doubt in court—certain other rights, equally important, are neglected. Notable among these is the right to self-defense. It is interesting to note that "The Rights of Americans," a collection of essays on individual rights published by Random House in commemoration of the 50th Anniversary of the American Civil Liberties Union, contains no mention of the citizen's right to protect himself from criminals, but "Rights of Suspects" is one of its longest treatises.

Speaking strictly in practical terms, it is good to be so discreet in the carrying of the gun that you neither show nor mention it to very many people. Keep your gun well hidden.

At the same time, if it is to be of value in the circumstances its very presence anticipates, it should be swiftly accessible to the owner. Even if you carry the gun just to feel secure in a dangerous neighborhood, how comforting is an emergency tool that can't be brought swiftly into play? A heart patient who keeps all his digitalis in the second floor medicine cabinet is not secure from a seizure in his basement.

The same holds true for guns. If the defense weapon is not actually available for swift defense, it is of little value as either a physical or a psychological security device.

The citizen who keeps a handgun for defensive purposes owes it both to himself and to bystanders to receive proper training, and practice frequently on a combat course.

Competency

If discretion is the most important thing to the man who carries a gun, competency is the most imperative to the man who eventually uses it. When you carry a defense gun, it is because you anticipate, however remotely, that you may be attacked in a public place. If this should come to pass, it is reasonable to assume that there will be bystanders present. Your competency with the weapon you carry must be such that you will not fire an accidental or panicky shot into a group of bystanders.

What frightens me most about civilians with guns is that so many of them are incredibly rotten pistol shots. The average man has learned to think of firearms as somehow magical: the gun is pointed in the general direction of he who is to be shot, there is a frightful flash and a jarring blast, and the victim falls.

It doesn't work that way. The handgun propels a small projectile in a relatively straight line. The layman should think of the gun as a high precision, remote-control drill. The bullet goes where it is aimed, not necessarily where it is wished.

There are too many people carrying guns they don't know how to shoot straight, guns they haven't fired in ten years. Faced with an attack that called for extreme response, they would probably jerk out the weapon, grasp it one-handed, and fire wildly from the hip, cringing from the unaccustomed recoil. There are people carrying guns they have never fired. Some policemen are in that category.

Contrary to public belief, there is a form of firearms control law that a few members of the "gun lobby" actively support: legislation requiring competency tests before the issuance of permits to carry concealed, loaded weapons. The very application for the carry permit indicates that the applicant believes that there is a chance, however remote, that he will some day have to use that gun in a tense situation in public. It is only fair, therefore, to require him to prove that he is capable of using his gun with precision under pressure (in this case, the stress of knowing that a poor score would cost him his pistol permit). I feel there should also be a written examination to determine his grasp of the laws that govern self-defense and deadly force.

A proper course might be 30 shots on the Colt Police Silhouette target, with the gun and ammunition the applicant intended to carry. It would differ from the standard police pistol course in that the maximum range would be shortened from 50 to 60 yards in the longest stages of the PPC, to 25 yards or less for civilians. The private citizen is less likely than the policeman to be involved in a long-range shootout. I would also eliminate the rapid reloading around which the police course is built: instances of armed combat involving civilians tend to be brief affairs, unlike the long gun battles a police officer must be prepared for.

Perhaps three sequences of 5 shots each at 7 yards (10 shots with the strong hand, 5 with the weak) would do to start, first in 15 seconds, then in 8. At 12 yards, two stages of five shots in 12 seconds each; and five at 25 yards in half a minute. The 25 yards is not an excessive distance. It is less than the length of a medium-sized bank lobby, or the breadth of a small parking lot. Nor are the time allotments a problem unless they are too easy. A passing score of 120 out of a possible 150 would be realistic; 70% is the police qualification minimum.

Competency tests now required in New York and elsewhere are not sufficient. There is no written exam on self-defense law, and no supervised marksmanship test. One need only find an instructor to sign his application.

Regular exams at the present permit-renewal intervals are indicated; they could be conducted like driver's tests, and just as quickly. It is argued that this would be impossible in view of the limited facilities. This is true of competency/marksmanship tests for hunters, of whom such an enormous number exist. But there are sufficiently few carry-permit holders that local ranges would be adequate to process them once each every one to three years. Small range fees could go to the host club owning the range to pay for the use of the facilities; where no civilian ranges exist, police facilities could be used, with the range fees going to fund the department's firearms practice budget. Alternatively, slightly increased range fees could pay for the supervisory services of gun-club or off-duty police instructors.

Chapter 12
High Price of
"Handgun Machismo"

Editor's Note:

GUNS magazine, of which the author is handgun editor, serialized "In the Gravest Extreme" prior to its publication in book form. When the chapter on common sense about guns on the street appeared, two angry readers accused Ayoob of cowardice and pacifism of vicious criminals, because of his mention that, sometimes, an attempt to casually "buy off" hassling rowdies could save a lot of present and future grief.

The following column in GUNS, in which Ayoob expanded on the buy-off tactic and commented on the common misconception that "When you carry a gun you don't have to take anything from anybody," received much acclaim from the readership. It is printed here with permission of GUNS magazine.

For some months now, GUNS magazine has been running a chapter per issue from my book, "In the Gravest Extreme: the Role of the Firearm in Civilian Self Defense." Most of the reader mail I've received has been quite gratifying. In another category, however, are two letters I've received from cops. I'm going to answer them in this column, not because they ticked me off and the journalist always gets the last word, but because the concepts they espouse show a frightening lack of understanding of how the criminal justice system treats law-abiding people who use guns in self defense.

Officer X, a New York cop with years on the street, and Officer Y, 27 years a patrolman and rangemaster in a northwestern city, both take vehement exception to the excerpt in which we discussed "A Gun on the Street." I mention that some people buy a gun with a blanket view toward self defense from anyone and anything, and start to feel, "With this on my hip, I don't have to take shit from anybody."

I took the example of a man walking with his wife, and being verbally harassed or even shoved by a group of foul-mouthed street punks. I explained that drawing a gun at that point would create a number of serious problems. I then stated that I carry a $5 or $10 bill wrapped around a matchbook, to throw to the harassers and say, "I don't want any trouble. Buy the guys a round on me." The reasoning is that (a) If I do wind up hurting someone, my attempt to buy them off looks great in court, and (b) it may satisfy their sick ego needs and prevent the situation from escalating. "It may be chicken, but it's worth it to me to keep from having to kill somebody."

I neglected to mention that I do this only when travelling out of state.

Well, Officer X and Officer Y clearly think that it *is* chicken. Officer X angrily cancelled his subscription to GUNS, and explained why in an articulate and heartfelt statement: he thinks that people like me contribute to the fact that street rats intimidate and extort old people and kids in New York.

Officer Y's approach was a bit more personal: he condemns me as a "true coward" who should turn in my badge before my yellow streak gets a brother officer killed.

OK, guys, I'm only gonna say this one more time, "In the Gravest Extreme" was written exclusively for *civilians* who lawfully keep or carry firearms for self defense. And its premise is what the title comes from: the lethal force of a handgun is only warranted when the citizen is *in the gravest extreme of immediate, unavoidable, deadly danger!* And that doesn't mean showing a bunch of smart alecs that you're a man, by waving a gun around.

Alternatives in between that and buying them off? Sure . . . you can reply in equally obscene language, or maybe deck one of 'em. If you do the first, you'll very likely wind up having to do the second anyway. Congratulations: you have just been provoked, or helped to provoke, a beef in which you are badly outnumbered. As they gang-beat you, you will doubtless realize that you're about to be maimed or killed, and will have little or no choice but to end the thing with gunfire, because you were so insecure about your own manhood, you had to prove it, "thus predictably escalating the conflict." That's what the court will say.

Want a precedent? In 1974, a midwestern policeman who was off duty walked into a bar for a quick brew. Three street punks of his professional acquaintance spotted him and began harassing him. I'd have bought them a round of drinks and tried to leave, ("true coward" that I am,) and marked the incident down in my accounts receivable column, to collect on at a more evenly balanced opportunity. This officer, a bit more to Officer Y's way of thinking apparently, responded like a real man. Yessirree. He wound up on the floor getting stomped by three pairs of engineer boots. Realizing that he was about to be killed or crippled, he drew his off duty gun and fired three shots. In moments, two of his attackers lay dead, the third paralyzed for life.

There was a fourth casualty: the officer himself. Exonerated by a department investigation, he was hauled into *civil* court for wrongful use of force. The judgment? Over $800,000.00 in damages. He fought it to the U.S. Supreme Court, and lost. When you figure what lawyer's fees add up to, you'll know that the $10 you tried to buy your attacker off with—thus helping to cement your claim in court that you tried every conceivable avenue of escape from the danger, including one personally humiliating to you—will stand you in better stead than any "expert testimony" you can get for $250 a day.

Impossible, you ask? *Baloney,* the court has answered. Yet the officer was about to be stomped to death! Sure. The court doesn't consider only the immediate circumstances of a self defense killing. *What led up to it will usually be found more important to the verdict.*

Why did that officer lose? A major reason was that the court felt he could have avoided the conflict, but made no effort to do so, thus violating one of the cardinal conditions you have to meet if you wish to exercise killing force within the law.

You think you're gonna snuff a street rat, and the Chamber of Commerce is gonna give you a Hero of the Year Award? Suuure ... but you're a lot more likely to get slapped automatically with a homicide charge. One of the most classically justifiable self defense killings I've ever run across happened two years ago. The guy who pulled the trigger is, at this writing, going into his second trial. The first one found him guilty of second degree murder. Right now, he's out of a job and has poured $27,000 into his court defense to date, not counting medical expenses for the ulcer that came along with the deal.

Where does injustice like that come from? Well, if you wind up in court on a murder charge, you'll find out that they don't call the American Way of Court "the adversary system" for nothing. It's a game between your lawyer and the prosecutor, to see who does his thing better, and *you* are little more than the stakes. And anything I, or Jeff Cooper, or Mason Williams, or anybody else ever told you about the principles of self defense will take a back-seat to that, and to the whims of the jury. And *that's* when you did everything within the letter of the law.

I should also add that I never have carried buyoff money while in any police capacity. I have done so as a civilian since 1972, but have never used it in any of the half dozen such confrontations I've been involved in since, partly because a little bit of me is perhaps into Officer Y's machismo trip, and partly because the situations were all such that either intimidation, or tactics and pre-preparedness, were working more effectively in my behalf.

Officer Y, I don't really give a damn if you think I'm a "true coward" because I said, "It's worth $5 or $10 to me (as a civilian) not to have to shoot anyone." When you figure that, if you're routinely booked for homicide, a typical bail will be $100,000 (and unless you've got that kind of cash rotting in Chase Manhattan's coffers, you'll have to pay the bondsman five or ten *thousand* that you'll never get back), I'll stand by that statement. And that's before you count up the frightful toll that even a justifiable homicide takes in lost friendships and jobs, shattered families, and smeared reputations.

Officer X, I sympathize with the tragedy of those victimized by extortionists. If they are prepared to defend themselves, and do so lawfully in the face of physical threat, I hope New York's prosecutors won't crucify them for it. Of course, you and I both know how few legitimate citizens in your city can *get* permits, and we both know what your city will do to them if they defend themselves with guns they *illegally* carry. And we especially know what New York would do to someone who pulled a gun in the face of "simple harassment," with no deadly danger yet apparent.

Officers X and Y, if you think I take any shit while behind my badge, your judgment of character is about as poor as your ability to distinguish tactics from cowardice. When I wear that shield, I've got a statute book that says a punk who disturbs the peace is *mine*, and his only option is whether he calls his lawyer from the police station or the emergency ward. But civilians don't have anything near that authority, and they don't realize how much trouble they can get into if they pretend they do.

Anybody reading this magazine who carries a gun for self defense had damn well better understand a few things quick, if he doesn't already. A gun is nothing more than a special-purpose item of emergency equipment, to be used only in the face of immediate and unavoidable danger of death or grave bodily harm to oneself or another innocent person. If you want to reinforce your self-image as a man, join a karate club or take up weightlifting. Both of those things will also be a lot better for your health. If you need something to make you feel masculine, suck on big cigars like Freud used to.

Second, while almost everything in print on the use of a gun for self defense begins with the draw and ends with the last shot, you have to understand that when it comes to court, the judge and jury will be looking at flashbacks from *long* before you went for your pistol, and the whole ordeal won't end for months or years, if ever.

Third, remember that when a person doesn't know the law, or has so little confidence in his manhood that he lets his machismo run away with his brains in a desperate effort to prove himself— and uses a firearm *outside the parameters of the law to do this*— he has endangered your right, and mine, to keep firearms for self defense against deadly danger. He has also kissed his own rights goodbye . . .

Chapter 13
Choosing a Gun for Defense

Revolver or Automatic?

We considered the relative merits of each type back in the chapter, "A Gun in the Store." To recap, the revolver is easier to manipulate, the automatic easier to shoot.

Among amateurs, it is said that the auto pistol is more likely to jam. The experts will tell you that the big automatics are actually more reliable than revolvers. This may be true—for the custom-tuned automatics the experts use.

The untrained civilian does not clean his gun regularly. A revolver will function in spite of this neglect. An automatic won't. The amateur keeps the pistol constantly loaded, with the same single magazine that came with the gun. Eventually, the compression of the magazine spring will cause metal fatigue, and the weakened spring won't feed the cartridges properly. Experts rotate their spare magazines every few months. To further reduce magazine spring stress, they will load the clip with one cartridge less than full capacity.

Let us look over the guns available. Space requirements limit our comments to the most popular models in each class.

The Snub-Nosed .38 Revolver

Some believe that the .38 snubby is a poor choice for the civilian, who probably can't hit anything with it. Actually, the snub-nose is the best all-around choice for a number of reasons. It is compact enough to be carried when bigger, easier-to-shoot weapons would be left at home. Also, it is small enough to be transferred to the pocket, where it may be held in discreet readiness. True, a full frame 4 inch barrel revolver is easier to shoot well, but the difference is not greatly significant at the point-blank ranges where most civilian shoot-outs occur. Choices include:

Colt's Detective Special. This is the best .38 snub-nose available. It is only slightly larger than the most compact models, has excellent sights and a full-length ejector stroke, and holds six shots. Two complaints: the fixed sights on the current guns tend to be out of line. This will be repaired by the factory or franchised dealer without charge, but it's an unnecessary annoyance.

Smith & Wesson's Chief's Special is the most popular .38 snubby. This is because most buyers hardly shoot these guns at all, and buy strictly on the basis of eye appeal. Those who use short .38's regularly in combat competition have found serious shortcomings in the little Smith. The sights are much too small. The ejector rod is too short to clear empties completely out of the chambers, a failing that can cause a fatal delay while reloading during a drawn-out gun battle. The sharply-squared cylinder release latch is so placed that, with a heavy-kicking Super Vel round, it can rip open the shooter's thumb. The small Smith & Wessons have a 5-shot cylinder squeezed into a frame designed for 6-shot .32's. The 5-shot cylinder is supposed to bulge less. Actually, there isn't that much difference in size.

On the plus side, finish is excellent and trigger action is the best of any snubby. Buy the all steel version, not the Airweights. The latter don't stand up well under continued heavy recoil, and their lighter weight is not noticeable when the gun is holstered. Better yet is the stainless steel version, the model 60. This gun will take much more abuse and neglect than the standard model, and for this reason is a good choice for the novice. But it will still rust if neglected long enough.

Smith & Wesson's Bodyguard is the Chief's Special with a built-in hammer shroud. Not as desirable as the shrouded Colt, in my opinion, since the latter can be detached to readily clean out the dust that accumulates inside the shroud.

Snub-nose .357 Magnums are built by Colt (Lawman) and Smith & Wesson (Combat Magnum). Both are substantially larger than the small frame .38's, and pay for their added power with vicious recoil. These are "experts only" guns, not for the ordinary armed citizen.

Service-Size Revolvers

Awkward to carry, they are easier for a novice to shoot accurately. "Kick" is noticeably less since weight dampens recoil. They have heavier frames and 4" to 6" barrels.

Smith & Wesson Model 10 Military & Police. The most popular service revolver, it's far and away the best in its class. The smooth double-action trigger pull is the standard by which other guns are judged.

The 4 inch heavy barrel is the choice of professionals. There is a two inch barrel available, but on this service revolver frame it is substantially bulkier than the other .38 snubbies. The model 10 is perhaps the only fixed-sight revolver that will shoot to point of aim as it comes from the factory. (The smaller Smith & Wessons tend to shoot low.)

Colt's Mark III Official Police and Lawman revolvers are a new design. Most experts consider the new action inferior to the old, which was more accurate and more reliable than the Smith in many respects. Adequate, but not especially recommended.

Colt's Police Positive is a small frame, four inch .38 Special revolver in between the snubbies and the service guns in terms of size and recoil. An ideal compromise for many.

Better Quality Revolvers

These are guns with slightly better finishes, smoother actions, and adjustable sights. All these are attributes that mean more to the enthusiast than to the average citizen who wants a gun for defense. The latter is, for instance, likely to screw up the adjustments on target sights anyway. Guns in this category include the Colt Diamondback (a deluxe Police Positive) and Smith & Wesson's Combat Masterpiece (a deluxe model 10).

.357 Magnums

These more powerful guns are, with the exception of the larger Smith & Wessons, built on medium .38 frames. Their recoil is heavy enough that it often outweighs the extra power, making the gun actually less effective for combat in the hands of the less experienced. The Smith & Wesson Combat Magnum and the Colt Trooper Mark III are comparable in every respect. The Dan Wesson revolver is not quite as well made, but is very sturdy (some 18 fewer moving parts than the equivalent Smith & Wesson). The action on the current model is much better than that of earlier Dan Wessons. The Ruger double action, rugged and smooth, is a fine value.

Service Automatics

With greater firepower and ease of shooting, these guns are excellent combat tools in the hands of one who keeps them clean and feeds them the right ammunition. As a combat weapon, the automatic's firepower—8 to 14 shots—and easy, rapid reloading make it superior to the revolver. Also, any of the guns listed in this section are more compact than the 4 inch service revolvers, and only slightly bulkier than the snub-nosed .38's.

Colt's Government Model is the standard .45 automatic. It has no double-action feature, and is best carried "cocked-and-locked," with a round in the chamber, hammer back, and thumb safety engaged.

This is frowned upon by some as being unsafe. This is so only when hammer and safety become worn or broken, and neither this nor any other gun is safe when in a state of disrepair.

The cocked and locked automatic is the fastest of any handgun for the first, aimed shot. The safety is naturally disengaged during the draw, as the thumb takes its position on the grips. Other guns can be fired just as fast, but *not* with the same accuracy at the same speed. This is because while the double-action guns require a long, 12-pound trigger stroke, the .45 or similar pistol is already cocked, and the short, 4-pound trigger pull is much less disturbing to aim. Thus, "the fastest *aimed* first shot."

The .45 holds seven in the clip and an eighth in the chamber. Unlike most autos, the magazine may be loaded to full capacity without sacrificing reliability of function. The big Colt and Browning pistols are generally considered the most reliable of automatics, due to the simplicity of design, and loose tolerances between parts.

"Kick" of the .45 is comparable to the .357 Magnum and is difficult to control without practice. The .45 is an experts only weapon, but in the hand of such an expert, it is an incomparable gunfighting tool.

The 10-shot Super .38 Government Model would be a superb weapon if soft-nose expanding ammunition were available. Since it isn't at this writing, it is not recommended for anyone but handloaders, who make their own suitable cartridges.

The Government model is also available in 9 m/m, but is not recommended in this caliber; the 14-shot Browning 9 m/m is a better choice.

Colt's Commander is a shorter-barrelled, alloy frame version of the Government Model. In .45 caliber, recoil is so severe that it cancels out the limited benefit of the weight reduction (26 ½ v. 39 oz.). A .45 is carried in a holster anyway, and weight difference is therefore negligible. The *Combat Commander*, a steel frame pistol, is a slightly shorter-barrelled Government Model. Choice between the Government model and the Combat Commander is strictly on personal whim. The lightweight Commander, however, is not recommended.

Browning's Hi-Power 9 m/m is noted for its 14-shot capacity (13 in the magazine, one in the chamber). Actually, you should only carry eleven or twelve in the clip, to save the magazine spring the stress that could impair its smoothness and certainty of feed. It is carried cocked and locked for fast use, like the Colt. Superb design and workmanship; very reliable. Author's choice in a 9 m/m automatic.

Smith & Wesson's Model 39 is highly popular, but some defects have shown up. The narrow, steeply angled feed ramp causes jamming with anything but full-jacketed bullets, which are poor stoppers for self-defense. (By contrast, the Browning will usually feed hollow points flawlessly, though some individual pistols do need throating.) The Smith & Wesson's alloy frame is not desirable in a combat automatic: weight adds recoil-stabilizing control, and the light Model 39 with sufficiently powerful ammunition kicks just as hard as the standard .45 while providing less stopping power.

Cartridge capacity is the same as the .45 (while the catalog says the 39 holds 9 rounds, it functions better with 8).

What sells the Smith & Wesson is the double-action trigger: like a revolver, the gun may be safely carried with a shell in the chamber, hammer down and safety off, and yet still be fired with a single pull of the trigger. There is less likely to be a failure in the safety system (or an accidental discharge by someone who "thought the safety was on").

The Model 39 is an attempt to make an idiot-proof auto pistol. The safety features are commendable, and would recommend it for an absolute novice who wanted an automatic—but the absolute novice would be better off with a simpler-to-operate revolver.

Watch out for the sights; Model 39's tend to shoot low.

Smith & Wesson's Model 59 is the above pistol with a 14-shot magazine. The double action is the same, as is the undesirable alloy frame. The 59 will be compared to the Browning Hi-Power: the 59 couples double-action with large magazine capacity; the heavier Browning is more controllable in rapid combat fire.

Colt plans to introduce a double action .45 and a double-action, stainless steel 9 m/m. Both will challenge the presently front-running models of semi-automatic defense pistols.

There are other models in this category, notably the SIG Neuhausen and Beretta 9 m/m's. Both are well made, particularly the SIG, but their safeties do not lend themselves to fast draw.

Rifles for Defense

High powered rifles are not recommended for self-defense. Designed for accurate, long range bullet placement, their only application in combat is as offensive weapons. Penetration and range are excessive in the event that the bullet misses entirely or passes through a gunman's body.

Many hunters rely on their deer rifles for home defense. They shouldn't. This writer has had occasion to fire a high-powered rifle in a closed room. The blast is literally deafening and stunning, like an explosion; it can disorient you for a few seconds at a moment when all your faculties *must* be functioning. Any gun fired indoors, even a .22, will make your ears ring, but a rifle's roar will render you unable to hear at all for some period of time. This can be fatal if you are stalking a hidden intruder through a darkened house, and must rely on your sense of hearing to locate him before he pinpoints you.

The only suitable rifle would be a fast-firing .22. This is easy for a novice to shoot with speed, and accuracy, and confidence.

A major problem with any rifle or shotgun is that it is too awkward to get into action quickly, or to handle in close quarters. A burglar will find it much easier to get a 3½ foot weapon away from you, than a pistol you can hold and fire with one hand.

Shotguns

The shotgun is the most devastating combat weapon available to the civilian. Police have found it deadlier than a submachine gun, unless the man with the latter has had special training.

Twelve-gauge is recommended. In a strictly defense weapon, the barrel should be 18 to 20 inches long, compared to 26 or 30 inches in a hunting gun. A barrel shorter than 18" brings the gun down into the illegal "sawed-off shotgun" category. 18 or 20 inch barrels, equipped with rifle sights and made for hunters who use shotguns for deer, are readily available.

Don't rely on a double-barrel shotgun. It *looks* frightening, but a one-or-two shot weapon is not something to rely on against even one opponent in a shootout. You don't know but what you'll be invaded by three or more. Only the 5-shot automatic or slide-action guns are desirable; these are the weapons police use as riot guns (usually the slide-action). Remington makes the best, smoothest, most jam-free slide shotgun. The Mossberg 500 has the best "human engineering" for a house defense shotgun.

For women, or other novices who find the pumping action of the slide awkward, an autoloading shotgun is a better choice. Get a gas-operated automatic, like the Remington 1100 or SKB which has less apparent recoil and is therefore easier on amateurs.

Some consideration should be given to ammo selection. One who can place his shots with rifle-like precision should use the heavy lead deer slugs. Their stopping power is unparalleled. Buckshot is the general choice; most favor the double-0 size, which in a 12-gauge will throw nine .33 caliber balls. Some have recommended birdshot, on the theory that at close range *any* shotgun blast is deadly, but birdshot won't carry far and is therefore safer. I prefer #1 buck, with 16 .30 cal. pellets.

Birdshot *is* devastating at point blank range, but even at a distance of 15 yards, a heavy coat will protect a gunman from much of the power of the shot. Stick with buckshot for defense.

The great advantage of the shotgun is its power, not the spreading pattern of its projectiles, but many novices have fallen victim to the "scattergun" myth that a man with a shotgun can hit anything that happens to be in front of the gun when the trigger is pulled. The pattern is actually much smaller than is generally believed. Try your shotgun out on a silhouette or similar target to get an idea of how it will perform at the ranges you anticipate. At 7 yards, the pattern will about cover the distance between two shirt buttons.

Definitely Not Recommended

Certain types of guns are simply unsuitable for gunfighting. These include single action revolvers, which must be thumb-cocked for each shot. Reloading is fatally slow, since each fired shell must be emptied, and each new one inserted, one at a time. Professional gunfighters considered these cowboy guns obsolete by the turn of the century.

Derringers are also inadequate. No gun that fires only one or two shots can be considered thoroughly capable of stopping even one homicidal attacker. Besides, the small-caliber ones are no smaller than a .22 or .25 pocket automatic, and the large caliber models are no more compact than a 7 or 8-shot .380. Finally, the old Remington-style design can go off accidentally if dropped; only Hi-Standard's .22 hammerless is safe to carry.

Cheaply made guns can get you killed. The little .22 revolvers that used to be sold mail-order for $15 bucks are now bought for $50 from Army-Navy and similar stores (never from gun shops, which refuse to carry them). Their parts are so soft that they deform after the wear of a few shots, throwing off the timing of the mechanism and causing misfires.

If you can't afford to pay for a new .38 Special, your best bet is a used weapon. Buy used guns only from gunshops, which depend for their livelihood on the satisfaction of their gun buyers, and which have the facilities to recondition used handguns before reselling them. Always testfire 50 or 100 rounds immediately after purchase, and bring the gun right back if it malfunctions. (Always test with the ammo you'll be carrying in the gun, since high-powered ammunition can create jamming problems that won't show up with mild practice loads. This is true of revolvers and automatics alike.)

A final note: because of space limitations, it is not possible to evaluate every firearm that could conceivably be used for defense. If your gun is not mentioned, it is not necessarily because it is undesirable, but because it is not among the front rank of either the most popular or the most suitable defense handguns.

Chapter 14
What Caliber for Self-Defense?

In selecting a cartridge for gunfighting, we must look for *shock power* or *stopping power*, not *killing power*. By shocking, stopping capability, we mean a bullet that delivers enough energy *at the very moment of impact* to make the man who takes the bullet immediately incapable of further assault, even to the extent of flicking his trigger finger. You want an impact that jars him, slams him backward, disorients him. The impact should numb his body, impairing his nervous system to the extent that his brain can no longer command his trigger finger to shoot.

There are two types of gunshot wounds. A large, heavy bullet has the most initial impact, and is therefore the most desirable. A standard .45 automatic bullet, for instance, will strike with the effect of a heavy punch.

A light, high-speed, expanding bullet will cause more damage than a slower, non-expanding .45. A 9 m/m, .38 Special, or .357 Magnum bullet does two things inside flesh: it expands to create a larger wound channel, and it causes a shock wave to ripple through the tissues surrounding the wound channel, breaking blood vessels and numbing local nerves. There is an element of a shock, caused mostly by the extensive internal damage and consequent heavy blood loss. But generally the "shock" of a light, fast, expanding bullet will not take effect as quickly as the "shock" of a wide, heavy bullet's initial impact. When we talk about "shock" in gunfighting parlance, we mean the initial jarring, knock-down blow, not the medical definition of shock as a slow-down of vital bodily functions following great blood loss or physical trauma. The "shock" of the high speed medium-caliber bullets is less immediate, but more fatal. This is due to the greater blood loss, and the likelihood that the criminal had to be shot several times when he didn't go down with the first hit.

A shopkeeper once asked me what kind of gun he should keep for defense. When I suggested a .38, he was outraged. "You'd *kill* somebody with that!" he shouted. "I just want to be able to *stop* them!" The bigger guns are actually *more* humane: a .45 automatic will usually neutralize a man with the first solid hit, and if the bullet has neither destroyed vital organs nor severed a major artery, and if he can be given proper care in time, he will survive. To be neutralized with a standard .38, he'll have to either be killed instantly, or hit with so many bullets that the blood loss and great tissue destruction will almost certainly be irreparable. I don't want to kill anybody, either. I *do* want to be able to instantly render a potential murderer incapable of killing *me*. That's why I carry a .45 when performing police duties.

Lesser guns will kill. They won't always *stop*. Small-caliber advocates will tell you that most cougar hunters use .22 pistols. They neglect to mention that the usual procedure is to tree the cougar, shoot him through the lungs, and let him bleed to death as he clings to the tree limb. A more powerful bullet would knock the cougar out of the branches, and down among the dogs who have treed him, and even in his death throes the big cat could rip a few of the dogs apart. It's still a rotten thing to do to the animal: if the hunter isn't capable of killing the beast instantly, and cleanly, he should leave it the hell alone. It's not a very smart thing to do to a criminal, either. He doesn't have to jump out of a tree to get you before he dies. All he has to do is twitch his trigger finger.

The best rule is to use the most powerful weapon you can control with speed and accuracy. There is a practical minimum, somewhere in the vicinity of .380 or .38 Special caliber, and there is a point on the other end of the scale, beyond which the blast and recoil of the biggest Magnums outweigh their awesome shock power.

No .32 caliber (7.65 m/m) cartridge has sufficient power to be reliable. Neither does the .38 Smith & Wesson round, known colloquially as the ".38 regular."

.380 Automatic

The .380 automatic cartridge (9 m/m Carto or 9 m/m Short) used to be lumped into the same category as the .32, but some tests have shown that the standard .380 is equivalent in stopping power to the .38 Special round-nosed bullet fired from a short-barrelled revolver. Neither bullet expands, and both penetrate to similar depths. Despite the great difference between the two on mathematically-formulated ballistics tables, they are comparable in actual performance.

Either gun will improve dramatically when high-speed, expanding bullets are used. With these loadings, the .38 Special gains superiority, since they can be loaded up to greater velocity. Super Vel's .380 gives good performance, but it's a bit hard on the guns. I don't use it in anything but a Walther or Browning and would never fire it out of older or weaker guns.

.38 Special

This revolver cartridge is often called the "police special" because it is used by 90-some-percent of American police. There has been a heated debate among many lawmen as to whether this is as it should be. Literally hundreds of shooting instances have shown that a gunman can take several .38 slugs in vital areas, and still keep coming. While some want .45's or Magnums, others point out that anything larger than a .38 is just too much for the average officer to handle with accuracy and confidence. The civilian who carries a .38 faces the same dilemma.

High-speed, hollowpoint ammunition greatly improves the .38 Special's performance; most of those failures to stop opponents occurred with the old slow, round-nosed, non-expanding bullets.

The hot ammunition will, however, produce vicious recoil and deafening muzzle blast in the snub-nosed guns. With alloy frame revolvers, this ammo is not recommended. The gun will be almost uncontrollable, since there is no weight to dampen the kick. The 110-grain hollow-points by Super-Vel, Norma, and others are the best choice for close-range civilian gunfights.

The flat-nosed, low-velocity .38 "wadcutters" used for practice, can be a good choice for women, due to the lesser blast and recoil. They may actually have *more* shock power than the standard round-nosed police bullet, for two reasons: the flat point hits harder and cuts a bigger wound channel than the round-nose (which tends to slip through muscles and other tissues, leaving a small hole), and the low-velocity bullet will be more likely to stop inside the criminal's body, without wasting shock power as does a slug that exits.

One warning, however: some people use .38 wadcutters in their home defense guns, on the theory that a miss will not penetrate the walls, endangering family members in other rooms. This is a fallacy; while penetration will be less than a higher-powered load, it can still go through several walls unless it hits a supporting beam. I was present at one shooting where a .38 wadcutter travelled through four walls and lodged in a window frame. Another half inch to one side, and it would have gone out the window and into an adjoining home.

.357 Magnum

Essentially a souped-up .38 Special, the Magnum has been greatly overrated. The increase in ballistic power is greater than the increase in actual shock power in living tissues. If a heavy bone is struck, the bullet will transmit its full energy; otherwise, it will pass through the body with little more effect than the .38 Special. Recoil, however, is substantially greater—usually more than the novice can handle. One very experienced police pistol instructor estimated that for every four fast, aimed shots from a .357, six can be delivered in the same time from a .38.[4] And this is with trained police officers. The Magnum's rate of accurate fire would be even less in the hands of a recoil-shy novice.

I do not recommend the .357 for untrained civilians. Even a man who can handle the recoil would be better off with a .45, which offers greater impact shock. The ideal .357 combat load is the 125-gr. hollowpoint. It has optimum penetration, relatively mild kick, and excellent shock power.

9 m/m Parabellum

The 9 m/m Parabellum, or Luger, is growing in popularity as a defense load more swiftly than any other. Its popularity is due more to the excellent weapons that come only in that caliber, than to the cartridge itself.

Roughly equivalent to a .38 Special in slide-rule ballistics, the 9 m/m is inferior in shock power in the standard loading. The fast, pointy, full-jacketed bullet just zips through tissues, leaving a tiny wound channel. High-speed expanding bullets, like the Super-Vel, are essential to make the 9 m/m a dependable combat weapon, *but they may not function properly without alterations to the pistol's feed system.* This is particularly true of the Smith & Wesson

---

[4]Weston, Paul B., "Police Combat Shooting," Springfield, Illinois: Charles C. Thomas, 1960.

Model 39 and 59. Remington, Federal, or Winchester 115-gr. hollowpoint is the only ammo to consider for self-defense.

People who buy 9 m/m's do so to get double-action trigger systems and 14-shot magazines, not because the cartridge itself is especially desirable.

The .38 Super

On paper, the Super is equivalent to the .357 Magnum. In reality, it is a poor choice as a combat weapon when factory, full-jacketed ammo is used. Like the standard 9 m/m, the Super bullet just drills a small, deep hole, transmitting little shock effect. Cartridges with expanding bullets are now available. Fine defense loads may be handloaded, of course, but this is not a consideration for those armed citizens who are not gun enthusiasts, and consequently buy all their ammunition off the shelf.

.45 Automatic

The .45 ACP (Automatic Colt Pistol) is a powerful round to control, but is considered by many to be the top self-defense cartridge. It normally comes with a round-nosed, full-jacketed bullet, which is generally considered inadequate. The .45 is the only pistol cartridge that has power enough to deliver massive shock in spite of the poor bullet design. This standard ammo, called "hardball," is recommended for the average .45 owner, since flat-nosed or hollow point bullets won't work with 100% reliability in many .45's unless the feed system is "throated-out" by a gunsmith so the edge of the flat bullet nose won't hang up going into the chamber.

One authority on defensive firearms, Jeff Cooper, has conducted exhaustive research on the relative shock power of .38-size guns as compared to the .45 automatic he favors. After analyzing a great many police gunfights, he found that the .38 would stop a criminal with a single, solid hit only about 50% of the time, while the .45 would do so in more than 90% of the instances studied. Nothing is 100%, but the .45 comes closer than any other handgun that is still controllable in rapid combat fire. For the man who can handle the recoil, which is about the same as a .357 Magnum, if not less, the .45 is the best choice for self-defense.

In a gun that will feed it reliably, hollow point ammo is a better choice in a .45. It magnifies shock power still further, while mitigating hardball's tendency to ricochet and, occasionally, overpenetrate.

.41 and .44 Magnums

These are the two most powerful cartridges made for currently-produced revolvers. The .44 Magnum revolver has, within 100 yards, shock power approaching that of a .30/30 carbine. The recoil is legendary, even among gun enthusiasts, and a person with limited training will find the weapon totally uncontrollable: fired with one extended hand in the target shooter's off-hand position, the gun rises above the shooter's head. A two-handed hold relieves the unpleasant shock of the "kick," but cannot prevent the muzzle lift.

This writer has qualified on the Police Pistol Course with a Smith & Wesson .44 Magnum loaded with Super-Vel. It can be done, but in the rapid-fire stages (i.e., 12 shots in 25 seconds, including reloading time), things get a bit tight; the gun must literally be pulled down out of recoil before it can be fired again. In a hairy gunfight situation, you may have to shoot much faster than you'll ever have to on the PPC, where a man who has learned to reload quickly can pretty much take his time.

The slow rate of fire caused by the heavy recoil can be fatal in a gunfight. If your first shot misses, or if you face two or more gunmen, you may be cut down before you can bring your Magnum back down to fire a second shot.

The .41 Magnum loading is pretty much the same story. There is a reduced power load for the .41 that is ballistically the same as the .45 auto, but recoil is much greater. The .44 Magnum was introduced for gun enthusiasts and big game hunters. The .41 was built to be a high-powered police gun, but failed as such because even trained cops couldn't handle the recoil. When San Francisco Police adopted the .41, qualifying scores dropped to 50%, compared to the 95% of the officers who qualified with the .38's. 'Frisco scrapped the .41 and switched to the .357 Magnum.

.22 Rimfire

The .22 long rifle cartridge has surprising killing power, but poor shock effect. The greasy, outside-lubricated bullet carries a lot of dirt into the body, creating a highly septic wound; the hollow-point bullet breaks apart and creates a great deal of internal damage; .22 slugs ricochet inside the body; the little high-speed bullets can even zip through some bullet-proof vests that would stop a .45. But there is no smashing impact. Those who have been shot with the .22 describe only a stabbing pain, with no numbing shock effect. Unless the bullet strikes the brain or spinal cord, the attacker will not go down. He is fully capable of killing you and walking away. That he may subsequently hemorrhage to death, or die from an infected wound, is of little consequence to the defender.

The same is generally true of .22 Magnum rimfire. It tears a bigger wound, but still has limited stopping power.

A .22 is a mouse-gun. It cannot be expected to sledge down a charging 200 pound attacker. Nevertheless, alone among small-caliber defense cartridges, it has a valid place as a self-protection weapon. This is because (1) it is easy for gun-shy amateurs to shoot rapidly and accurately. There is no vicious recoil or deafening blast to make them cringe, close their eyes, and jerk the trigger; wild shots are therefore made less likely. There is a more subjective factor involved here. A person who is afraid of his gun will never be able to effectively defend himself with it in a gunfight. He won't even be able to make a convincing threat, because the criminal he holds a gun on will probably sense his uncertainty.

(2) The main reason most gun-carrying private citizens—and for that matter, so many policemen—are such lousy shots, is that they don't practice. Some are just disinclined, while others rely on the magic power of the gun to drop anything that is anywhere in front of it when it goes bang. But the main reason is, "I can't afford twelve dollars a box to practice with every month!" "Remanufactured" ammo for .45's, 9 m/m's, and .38 Specials are available at as little as $5 per box of 50.

By contrast, a box of 50 .22's can be had for a little more than a dollar. This encourages practice, which is essential to one who wishes to be able to protect himself (both from armed criminals and from lawsuits by innocent bystanders hit by wild shots).

The .25 Automatic

Not recommended. This round has even less potency than the .22 hollow-point, which at least causes enough internal damage and bleeding to slow him up over the course of a drawn-out gunfight involving barricaded combatants. The .25 has *no* stopping power. If I had to defend myself with one, I would violate a basic gunfighting rule and aim for the head.

Even this won't always work. I know a man who was shot point blank in the left temple by a bandit with a .25. He turned around, drew his .38 Chief's Special, and was about to kill him when he was clubbed from behind by another robber. The bullet had struck at a slight angle, skidded down the outside of his cranium through the inside of his ear, and emerged through his neck. He recovered completely. Another friend had a .25 slug skid off his temple; he then shot down both attackers.

The only advantage of the tiny .25 is that it is convenient enough to be carried when a .38 might be left at home. "A .25 is a nice thing to have when you're not carrying a gun."

Seriously, a properly worn .380 or .38 snubnose can be worn discreetly under any dress code short of a nudist colony's.

Chapter 15
Basic Gunfighting Technique

Throughout this book, we have mentioned the various techniques of survival relevant to the particular situation being discussed. Let us now look at some of the basics.

Quick Draw

The fastest draw is to have the gun in your hand before the fighting starts. The second fastest is a high ride, straight-draw holster under the gun hand. I don't care for the "break-front" holsters, where the gun is pushed out through the front rather than pulled out through the top. It looks fast, but when you actually use one, you find yourself pushing against a heavy spring-tension that releases suddenly; it makes for an awkward, uneven drawing motion.

The cross-draw holster—on the side opposite your gun hand, butt forward—has certain advantages. It's easy to reach with your weak hand, and easy to get at between the buttons of a closed jacket. To keep it in reach, however, you'll have to wear it well forward of the hip. In this position, it will be visible the moment you unbutton your jacket. Also, the butt-forward gun is in an ideal position to be snatched by anyone standing in front of you. In any case, you will have to swing the gun across a 90-degree area to bring it to bear on your opponent.

In a straight-draw, the gun comes up naturally onto the opponent since you are probably facing him anyway. The actual drawing motion itself is faster. In cross-draw, the hand reaches across the body, stops, grabs the gun, and swings back. In straight draw there is a single continuous motion: the hand describes a circle as it swings smoothly back up, catching and withdrawing the gun as it comes up naturally into line with the target.

Shoulder holsters are drawn from in much the same way as cross-draw belt rigs. With a conventional shoulder rig, you'll reach up and over, drawing the gun down and out; with an "upside-down" holster, your drawing hand goes up and in, down and out. The latter is faster and more natural.

Suffice to say that the professional gunfighters—the felony squad cops—use the straight draw almost exclusively.

One thing I teach in my firearms classes is to leave the finger out of the trigger guard until after the weapon clears the holster. This is for two reasons: the finger has been mentally programmed to squeeze the trigger, and if the gun hangs up in the holster, the gun may be discharged prematurely. Also, the extended finger "points" naturally toward the target as the gun comes up, insuring that it will rise into line naturally. As the gun comes up, the finger goes into the guard and onto the trigger. This is awkward for beginners, but becomes instinctive with practice.

Position

A black belt judoist who taught unarmed combat to thousands of cops and went on to become chief of police in a good-sized city, once told me his philosophy of teaching weaponless defense to rookies: "If you show them six ways to pin a man, they'll never learn any of them properly in the short time you have for training. I teach them one good come-along hold, and make them practice 'til they have it down pat. A man who has *mastered one* approach is more formidable than one who has been 'exposed' to many."

The same principle holds true in the scientific art of gunfighting. To explain every possible draw-and-fire sequence would require a whole book in itself. Thus, we shall select the most effective single stance: the two-handed erect position.

"The gunfighter's crouch" is the classic shooting position. It needn't be. The crouch takes a precious split-second to move into, and is an awkward position for the beginner to assume. The main purpose of the crouch is to make you a smaller target, and to make you better able to absorb a bullet: since your weight is balanced forward of your flexed knees, you will probably fall forward if hit. At close range, you can return fire better if you fall on your back. On the other hand, master gunfighter Bill Jordan feels that the man who stays erect, and draws his gun that much quicker, will get in the first, deciding shot and won't have to worry about where he should have fallen if wounded.

Jim Cirillo, a police firearms authority who blew away eight men in eight gunfights and never took a bullet himself, told me that he never crouched when he fired: he stood up straight, held the gun in both hands, lined up the sights deliberately, and killed the criminals who were shooting at him from the hip.

This lining up of sights is ignored by most "gun experts" who advocate instinctive shooting. Actually, it is essential to do so: hip-shooting can only be done with accuracy by a highly-trained, well-practiced man. The hard-learned coordination between hand and eye that enables a trick shooter to hit tiny targets, just won't function under the stress of mortal combat. It takes only an extra split-instant to bring the gun up to eye level, and to bring the weak hand up to support it. It's not the first shot that counts, but the first *telling* shot. To place that first deciding bullet any gunfighter will need the added control of the two-handed, standing, aimed position.

At point blank range, you may have to start as soon as your gun clears leather. Practice from this position until you can correct the natural tendency to shoot low. But most of your practice should be in the two-handed standing position, increasing the speed of fire as soon as you can while retaining accurate delivery. Ultimately, you will be able to put every bullet into the X-Ring of a Colt silhouette target at 7 yards, firing as fast as you can pull the trigger.

Practical Hints

If it looks as if a gunfight is in the offing, have your gun in your hand before the shooting starts.

Always take advantage of cover. Never issue a "drop your gun" challenge to an armed offender; shoot him where he stands. If you are not sure he is armed, ensconce yourself behind substantial cover before you give away your position. He may turn and try to shoot you to death. Cops don't call the verbal warning a "challenge" for nothing.

If you have to shoot a man, keep shooting until he is either unconscious, dead, disarmed, or so torn apart that he can't function. A major fallacy is that the criminal will fall with the first bullet. He may take a clipload before he goes down, and if you wait for him to fall after the first hit, you may get shot yourself. Keep firing 'til he can't shoot back.

Some states consider it an indication of murderous malice to shoot a man who has fallen. This does not hold true if the fallen criminal still has a gun in his hand. A dying thug can still take you with him. A lot of cops and law-abiding citizens alike have lost their lives because they shot a criminal once, and just stood there waiting for him to fall down.

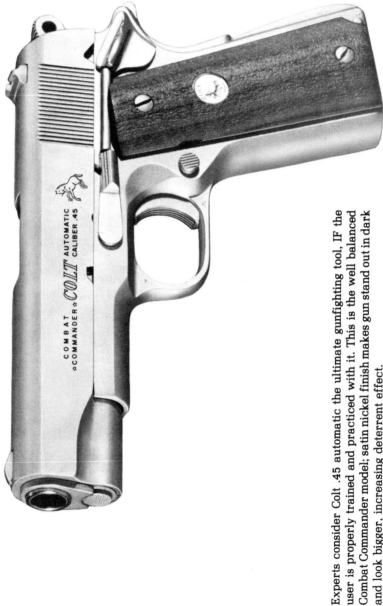

Experts consider Colt .45 automatic the ultimate gunfighting tool, IF the user is properly trained and practiced with it. This is the well balanced Combat Commander model; satin nickel finish makes gun stand out in dark and look bigger, increasing deterrent effect.

Point of Aim

Go for the center of the chest. The head is a small target, and its internal helmet of bone can deflect a bullet that strikes on an angle.

Never shoot for the abdomen. It is the biggest target, but a hit there causes only pain and sometimes lingering death, *not* the immediate nullification you're aiming for, unless you have an extremely potent gun.

We shoot for the center chest because it's the biggest target that can be expected to cause immediate nullification when hit. Contrary to popular belief, a heart shot does not necessarily cause instant death. A bullet in the brain or spine is an "instant stop," because the nerves that command the body to fight are immediately short-circuited. The heart is *not* immediately necessary to physical activity: the body can function for several seconds after the heart has stopped beating. A man can take a .38 slug through the heart, and empty his gun before his blood pressure falls.

But the center chest target is vital and easy to hit. It's the point to aim for. *But keep shooting until your assailant is obviously unable to shoot back.*

Taking a Bullet

You may be shot yourself in the course of a gunfight. The sensation will depend upon where you are hit, the power of the slug that nailed you, the way you are standing, your state of mind, and several other variables.

Expect pain, breathlessness, and a sensation of impact. There will probably be a burning sensation in the area of the hit. Overriding all of this will be a nightmarish sensation of terrifying, unnatural hurt as your body screams to your brain, "there is something horribly, frightfully wrong!"

Ignore it, and keep shooting. You have to. If you fall, your opponent will probably put a bullet through your brain before he leaves the scene.

First-aid for puncture wounds would take another whole book. Sign up for the next first-aid course the Red Cross sponsors in your community, and keep first-aid kits in your car, store, and home. Gunshot victims should be treated for shock and hemorrhage.

Remember above all that the thing that kills innocent people in gunfights is their own morally-inbred hesitation to kill fellow beings. It is not a consideration shared by the criminals the private citizen may someday face.

Practice

You owe it to yourself, and to the innocent people around you, to be able to deliver your self-defensive gunfire into the vital organs of the criminal who gravely threatens you, and nowhere else. Certain gunowners who read this book will want to kick my ass because I suggest competency tests for people who wish to carry firearms. So be it. But competency is essential for those who wish to protect themselves from criminal assault that they can protect themselves from in no other way. A man who can't control the deadly force of his gun adds to the general jeopardy; a man who can use it effectively to eliminate vicious, professional criminals, reduces that far-reaching threat.

Practice is essential. I shoot once each Wednesday as the captain of a first-string league pistol team; in season, I shoot every weekend in combat tournaments, in the pressure of the knowledge that I am shooting in competition for money and trophies. It's the best kind of conditioning. While the civilian is not eligible for most combat shoots—the NRA, which sponsors police combat matches, expressly forbids civilians to shoot at the human-shaped targets—pistol competition is nevertheless the quickest avenue to competency. The tension of competition is the closest artificial approximation of the pressure involved in a real shootout. Free-style combat shooting, gunfight simulation at its best, *is* open to civilians.

Even if you shoot at silhouette targets at a remote sandpit range, you face a unique social problem: people driving by will call the police and say, "There's a crazy person in the sandbank shooting at pictures of people." Legitimate as it is, it looks bad.

Regular bullseye pistol shooting is socially acceptable. The principles learned there are remote from gunfight situations, but still carry over into the latter application. Certain combat shooting authorities say that only silhouette targets are relevant for gunfighting practice, that the ability to drill bullseyes is meaningless.

Bullshit. In summer of 1972, an auxiliary police pistol team was

117

formed by myself and three other men who were, in civilian life, veteran bullseye target shooters. Within three months, we had captured three state championships in police combat pistol matches. Even though the best practice is that which simulates combat situations, the skills learned in target shooting do apply to real life circumstances. Regular participation in combat shooting tournaments is even more relevant: the police officers of my acquaintance who have survived the most gunfights are regular, top-scoring competitors in combat pistol matches. The cops who hold the highest "Kill Records" in two of America's largest police departments are regular competitors in both bullseye and combat pistol tournaments.

Rapid Reloading

Most civilian gunfights are of brief duration. Unlike the police officer, who is duty bound to pursue fleeing criminals, the private citizen will seldom be involved in a running gun battle. It may happen, however, that after the initial exchange of fire, the surviving assailants may take cover instead of escaping.

If the shootout is thus prolonged, you will have to reload your weapon immediately. A criminal a room away who hears the click of the gun opening may realize that you are defenseless at that moment, and renew the attack then. Reloading speed is therefore imperative.

Speed of reloading is one of the auto-pistol's great advantages: one simply withdraws the depleted magazine and inserts a fresh one. If the gun is empty, the slide will usually lock back; when the new clip is inserted, the slide is released either by a hand motion or by pressing the slide-release button, which is situated next to the tip of the right-handed shooter's thumb. It is now ready to go. *One should not, however, wait to reload until the automatic is empty.* Even if you have fired only three or so shots, you should put in a full clip at the first lull in the shooting.

Some pistols, notably the Browning and Smith & Wesson 9 m/m's, have magazine disconnector safeties: the gun cannot be fired unless the magazine is fully inserted. This is to prevent accidents in the hands of thoughtless people who remove the magazine to empty the gun, but forget the round in the chamber. In a combat situation, however, it is desirable to be able to fire that chambered round if you are jumped while reloading.

A revolver is much slower to reload: one must open the cylinder, eject the empties, and insert a fresh cartridge in each chamber. This takes the seasoned combat shooter 10 to 12 seconds, while the novice requires half a minute or more.

You should follow this sequence: holding the gun in your right hand, open the cylinder, then hit the ejector rod a single sharp blow. Hold the weapon vertical so the empties will fall out easier. It is at such a moment that you will appreciate a full-stroke ejector rod: the short rods of snub-nosed Smith & Wesson and Charter .38's, and the Ruger Security-Six, may not clear the empties all the way. The time it takes to pick each fired casing the rest of the way out of the chamber can cost your life in a gunfight if your opponent jumps you as soon as he hears you open the gun.

If you carry your spares in your pocket, they should be on your right side. While your left hand cups the gun under the cylinder, drop the fresh ammo into your left palm, and load them one by one. If you try to load them two-at-a-time, or load them with the same hand that's holding the rest, you'll drop them sure as hell.

You can load from the belt with a 6-shot loop carrier like the Hume. If you buy another brand, make sure the loops are on the top edge of the carrier so you can get at the cartridges without fumbling. The loop should be worn on the front of your belt, not in the back. Avoid belt pouches: they are both bulkier and slower than the loop-type.

The only "speed loader" compact enough to be carried in plainclothes is Bianchi's speed strip. If you follow the manufacturer's instructions, you'll drop some of the cartridges. The strip is much easier to manipulate with only 5 rounds. It's fast, but tricky: you have to stay in practice to use it smoothly. For the average revolver owner, I recommend the Hume belt-loop carrier.

Everyone who carries a sidearm should have at least one gunload of reserve ammunition on his person. The automatic user should carry the spare clip in a pouch, like the Bianchi which hooks onto the belt. A magazine in the pocket will pick up dirt and lint, which will cause malfunctions.

Double Action Shooting

The long, heavy pull of the double action trigger is not conducive to accuracy. It's hard to keep a two-pound gun in line when you're exerting 12 pounds of pressure on it. This is why so many cops are such lousy shots with their double-action revolvers.

119

Amateurs make two mistakes with double action triggers: they make the whole pull in a single, jarring jerk, or they pull it back over its 1/2''–3/4'' of travel with a series of nervous little twitches. They can't hit anything either way.

Experts use one of two double-action techniques. They either complete the pull in a single smooth, rolling motion, or they "brake" the trigger. The latter system involves bringing the trigger almost all the way back, then bracing the top of the index finger on the thumb or pistol grip, and squeezing off the last couple of pounds of pressure as with a single action pull. Either way will take a full second or more. As practice and expertise increase, the trained double action shooter learns to pull the trigger as fast as he can while retaining this smooth, controlled motion. You can soon reach 6 "kills" in 1-1/4 seconds with a .38.

Chapter 16
Gun Safety

The standard basic rules of firearms safety are worth repeating here: Never point a weapon at anyone or anything you are not prepared to shoot. Treat every firearm as if it were loaded. Never play with guns; fast-draw practice and dry-fire drills should be conducted *only* after making doubly certain that the gun is not loaded, and should always be undertaken with the same seriousness as live-ammo practice. Check and clear *every* weapon, every time you pick it up. Keep all guns in proper working order.

For those who keep or carry loaded guns for protection, we may add the following caveats: *Never* leave a potentially deadly weapon where unauthorized hands may find it. *Never* insert your finger into the trigger guard until the actual use of a weapon seems imminent; a fall, or the muscle-tightening reaction to a sudden noise, can result in an accidental discharge. *Never* keep a loaded gun on display, especially in a case alongside unloaded arms. *Never* touch a firearm while under the influence of alcohol, or display one at an occasion when liquor is flowing, (*never* take a gun into a bar or cocktail party). *Never* allow yourself to become embroiled in a squabble while you are carrying a gun, be it caused by an insult to your wife, an argument in traffic, or any similar situation. *Never* let it be known to anyone outside your immediate household, or outside those associates in the profession that requires you to, that you carry a gun. *Never* make remarks to the effect that you will "kill any sonofabitch who breaks into my house/hooks my kid on drugs/tries to steal from my store," etc. If such a killing situation ever occurs, testimony in court will show that you seemed pre-occupied with the idea of killing real or imaginary criminals, especially if you've made such remarks frequently. If circumstances were such that your reactions could be considered to have been too hasty, such testimony would imply that you were excessively pre-disposed toward using your gun.

Keeping Guns in the House

There are no set safety rules for keeping a loaded gun in the household, only the obvious necessity of keeping them out of the hands of those unauthorized and/or unqualified to touch them. We are talking mainly about children.

There are two approaches: the gun may be secured in such a manner that it can be reached only with great difficulty, or the children may be educated in such a manner that you can be sure they won't touch them without your permission. A combination of both is generally desirable, with emphasis on the first approach for very small children, the second for those more mature.

There is no such thing as a childproof firearm. I recall that, at the age of four or five, I was able to operate my father's handguns (under his supervision, of course). While I was not strong enough to draw back the slide of an automatic pistol, I *could* release the safety and pull the trigger. While I could not pull a double action revolver trigger, or cock the hammer with my hands, I *could* cock one by holding it in both hands, and pushing the hammer back against the edge of a table.

What my father emphasized to me, though, was how I could *neutralize* a pistol or revolver. He showed me how to withdraw an automatic's magazine, and lock the thumb catch on safe. I learned how to open the latch of a revolver's cylinder, and punch out the cartridges. At the same time, it was made thoroughly clear that the guns were not to be touched except in his presence. The loaded guns he showed me were in his jewelry store; he did not permit loaded firearms in the house until I, his youngest, was eleven and already had my own first handgun.

It was, in retrospect, an ideal system. He at once satisfied the two basic imperatives of teaching children about guns: teach him to stay away from yours, and teach him to cope with the situation if, through his own failure in judgment or that of a playmate, he finds himself in proximity to a loaded firearm.

While you can educate your own offspring in relation to your own guns, you have no control of the manner in which his playmate's father has trained *his* kid. While you're in the process of teaching your son the rules about your guns, spend a little more time and give him the knowledge he will need if he is ever in a friend's house, and the other kid pulls out the loaded .38 his father doesn't think he knows about. Instruct your kid that if this ever happens, he should tell the other kid to put it away or he won't play with him, and then split at the first opportunity. He is to tell you or your wife immediately. If the other youngster insists on playing with it, have your son trained to say, "Hey, point it down to the floor, and let's open it and see if it's loaded." If your son is familiar with the mechanism, he can then unload or otherwise neutralize it (but impress upon him that if it's *not* like one of yours, he is not to touch it!). If this also fails, teach him to remain calm and leave on the first possible pretext. He should *never* try to take the gun away from the other boy by force, or suddenly run away (the child with the gun, who obviously isn't too bright or too well-disciplined, may angrily aim it at him and pull the trigger).

Unless your child is mentally or emotionally disturbed, the only reason he will take one of your guns out is to (a) impress his friends, or (b) satisfy his natural curiosity—he is, after all, growing up in a society where heroes with guns dominate his major sources of entertainment.

Both motivations can be dealt with by a concerned and enlightened parent. A child who wants to enhance his standing among his peers with the display of a demonstrably "adults-only" object, can be satisfied in a controlled manner: teach him or her firearms safety and marksmanship, and buy him an inexpensive .22 rifle with the stock cut down to fit. If he wants to impress a friend, allow him to invite the kid along with the two of you on a Sunday afternoon plinking session (with the approval of the guest's parents, of course).

As far as satisfying the child's natural curiosity about guns, there is no reason not to let the youngster handle the unloaded weapon in your presence—the very defense pistol you usually keep loaded, not a .22 rifle or other less fascinating weapon. Better yet, teach him how to clean the gun: it will at once save you a tiresome job, and give him a safe familiarity with the gun.

Do not believe for a moment that you can keep a gun in an accessible place without his knowledge. There are few items in your house that your children have not found and curiously examined, with or without your knowledge. So long as you have impressed upon him that he is not to touch the weapon without your supervision—and have removed his desire to do so by satisfying his curiosity—he'll probably avoid it. Even if he does touch it without permission, he at least knows enough about its operation to minimize the chance of an accidental discharge. There is no safety in ignorance.

There is no set age at which a child can or should be exposed to firearms. Maturity is not measured in years, and the parent himself is the best judge of the given youngster's judgment and responsibility. Some are ready at five or six, while some will never be trustworthy with guns (or with automobiles, or alcohol, or other things that are safe and of constructive use only in the hands of rational, responsible people).

I know children of eight that I would, and do, trust to walk behind me with a loaded shotgun in a game field. I also know highly trained veteran police officers so irresponsible with firearms that if I walked into a gunfight situation alongside one of them, my first impulse would be to get out of his line of fire.

If all your children are not mature enough to be trusted around guns, the weapons should be locked away, and the only keys held by you and your wife. One method is to keep the loaded gun in a locked drawer, with the keys on dog-tag chains around the neck. Or, the drawer can be kept locked all day, unlocked upon retiring, and locked again when the parent(s) leave in the morning.

A common practice is to keep an automatic pistol, either unloaded or with the magazine in and the chamber empty. To draw back the slide against the heavy spring tension to chamber a cartridge and cock the hammer, is almost impossible for a small child. For *how small* a child? Physical strength development does not always relate directly to age. Once a year, make double-sure the gun is empty and hand it to each gun-trained child, challenging them to pull back the slide. It's the only way you'll know for sure. A revolver is not childproof, not even the Smith & Wesson hammerlesses with their grip safeties and extra-tough trigger pulls.

In a long gun, almost any mechanism can be operated by a child who can figure out a way to balance a bulky gun and hold it in place while he works the bolts and levers. A pump shotgun is supposedly the safest, since having been pumped on an empty chamber, the action locks until an inconspicuous button is pressed, and the now-unlocked slide forced back to chamber a shell. This is fallacious, however; a kid can simply snap the trigger, unlocking the slide mechanism. Let it be repeated: *no gun is childproof.* No matter how many levers and buttons it has, the child will eventually figure out the combination.

In a non-defensive atmosphere guns and ammo should of course be locked away separately. But I have interviewed shaken homeowners after housebreaks, and believe me, the achingly long fumbling for the locked up gun and cartridges can be a nightmarish experience when the invader's footsteps are rapidly ascending the stairs.

I'll go with a .45 automatic, with an extra-heavy spring and charged with heavily handloaded ammo that will function with the stiffer spring. For the non-specialist, a factory automatic with factory ammo is probably the best compromise.

Another possibility is a loaded revolver with a safety lock fitted to the trigger, and the key kept on the person, as with a locked drawer. The best safety device is the Bor-Lok, which extends a rod through the barrel and empty chamber and is released by a combination lock that protrudes from the muzzle (be sure you've memorized the combination). All such gun locks are available from hardware and sporting goods stores.

If you do not have children in the home, you have much greater latitude in the keeping of weapons. *Bear in mind, however, the possibility of a guest's child finding them.* There are no small children in my own home at present, but friends and relatives with little ones of course drop in. Regular visitors who bring youngsters have been requested to call beforehand so that either my wife or I can remove all firearms from sight and reach. This is still done even when the visit is a surprise. Since much of my work involves firearms, a number of them are constantly lying about, and their presence is not only an unnecessary temptation to youngsters but a source of discomfort to adults who are not accustomed to firearms.

When the household is child-free enough to give you some latitude, you'll have a choice of several accessible locations in which to place your defense gun.

Never put one under your pillow. It will shift around beneath it as you move about in sleep, and you'll have to grope for the damn thing when you need it. Also, there's something "not-quite-right" about it; most of us associate the practice with paranoids and hoodlums.

Another danger is something that could happen during a nightmare. There are certain motions that the body actually carries out in a dream-active sleep, and if you're having a particularly intense and realistic nightmare involving a gunfight, it's just as well that your bedroom pistol be out of immediate reach at that moment. Relatively few people have such extreme physical response to dreams, but those who have don't know it, never having been awake to notice.

If you sleepwalk, forget about keeping a loaded gun.

* * * * *

Getting down to terms of practical accessibility to the loaded weapon, night table drawers are out. The thing you have to remember is the possibility of the very worst contingency—the intruder has already entered your bedroom before you awake.

He will, if he's looking for a weapon, go for the bedside drawer first, then the headboard of the bed. He'll probably look under the pillow, too, since if he thinks you may be armed, this is the classic place he'll expect to find the weapon.

Some people keep their guns between the mattress and the box springs, on the theory that this is one place the kids won't look for it. It's also the last possible place you'll get it out from if the bedsprings are compressed under your body, or of the combined weight of an assailant who may be strangling you.

Night table drawers and the compartments of headboards are convenient and discreet, but in this one situation—the invasion of the sleeping quarters—they are useless, since your attacker will never permit you to reach these locations.

Perhaps the optimum location is beneath the bed. The gun in this position is readily and silently available, and is accessible in that extreme situation of being attacked while in bed. In that case, one simply rolls sideways toward the floor, and grabs it from there.

The gun should be protected from dust by keeping it either in a shoebox, or between the pages of what an observer would see as a casually-dropped magazine.

Chapter 17
The Aftermath

Let us suppose that the unlikely events considered here have come to pass: you have been compelled to kill in defense of yourself, your family, or other innocent persons.

Your first act should be to call an ambulance; your second, to call the police.

Expect to be arrested and charged with murder. Most statutes stipulate clearly that the perpetrator of any homicide be charged with murder, unless the evidence of the prosecution (i.e., the decision of the police investigators) obviously indicates that the killing was justified.

Explain to the arresting officers that you're not a punk taking the Fifth, but you'd rather wait until you spoke with your attorney before making an official statement. Call your attorney as soon as you've notified the police and emergency units.

MAKE NO STATEMENTS WHATEVER TO THE PRESS. Newsmen have found that murder sells more papers than justifiable homicide, and shooting incidents tend to become distorted by the time they reach the printed page. You may think that you'll be treated like a hero for killing a criminal. You're probably wrong. Two cases in point:

—An elderly man is arrested for the murder of a youth. The front-page story describes a young boy shot to death by an old man, after the kid participated in a noisy gathering in a public area below the old man's window. It appears from the news story that a crazy old man had shot a kid for making noise in the street. Some time later, a short blurb in the back of the paper tells the real story: the kid had been participating in a gang rumble, had smashed through the French doors into the living room of the apartment that overlooked the rumble scene, and was already in the living room when the terrified old man shot and killed him.

—A New Englander is arrested for shooting to death two young men who were passing by his house during the hunting season. A front-page picture shows the handcuffed man being led to a patrol car, trying to avert his face from the camera. When it is learned that he was released on bail, the public cries, "My God, they let the crazy bastard go after he murdered those two kids?"

Later, those who read the newspapers all the way to the back will learn what really happened. Two punks had driven by the man's house, stopped, and out of sheer viciousness had sicced a German Shepherd on his wife and his tiny dog. They got out of the car themselves, drew knives, and followed the terrified couple to their front door. When the homeowner produced a .22 rifle and both threatened and begged them to leave, they laughed in his face and kept coming. He shot them. One fell across the doorstep, the knife still in his hand. The wrap-up appeared in a tiny section of the same paper that had headlined his arrest.

The reaction of the press can destroy your life and that of your family. The paper usually can't be held liable: they reported the news that was available to them at the time of your perfunctory arrest.

Consider, too, the merchant who shoots a black-masked figure who was pointing a gun at him. When he and the investigating officers approached the corpse, they find a dead teenager with a realistic looking cap pistol clutched in his hand. Yes, it was justifiable; the storekeeper who pulled the trigger was in reasonable fear of his life. But suppose the morning headlines reads, "Boy With Toy Pistol Slain by Merchant." Justifiability aside, do you think that businessman will ever make a living in that community again?

Even the most justified killing of the most despicable criminal can be made to appear unjust. The citizen must never delude himself that the shooting of a lawbreaker will make him a hero. Consequently, he has another reason to use his legal gun only to escape death or grave bodily harm, only when the consequences of submitting to the criminal are deadlier than the potential consequences of taking that criminal's life.

Liability

A common question is, "What if I shoot at a robber and hit a bystander instead?" In many states, such an accidental shooting is treated by the statutes as if the bullet had hit the intended target. A bullet aimed to murder will be treated as murder if it kills a bystander; a shot aimed at a criminal will be justifiable or excusable if it hits an innocent party. So the statutes say, anyway, but read them carefully. Pay particular attention to the mention of negligence as a factor in unintentional homicide. *If it can be proven that you were negligent or reckless in firing the wild shot, you are liable for damages, and for conviction under the criminal code.* And nothing is more negligent than shooting a deadly weapon at one person and hitting another.

If the shot went awry because the suspect jarred your arm or something, he is responsible for the innocent person's injuries. Otherwise, it's in *your* lap. And don't count on your liability insurance policy if you're sued for an awesome amount. If the court finds that there was criminal negligence on your part, they are excused from paying claims. It is now *you* who must bear alone the medical and suffering costs awarded to the bystander hit by your bullet. The same is true if he was hit during a gunfight that took place only because you followed an escaping armed robber out in the street and there engaged him in combat: whether the wild shot was his or yours, it was you who carried the gunfight from a private establishment to a public place, you who set the stage for the innocent person to be needlessly shot.

*   *   *   *   *

It is axiomatic that those who legitimately carry guns are seldom the ones who have need to employ deadly force in self-defense. There is something in the bearing of an armed man that discourages would-be attackers, and there is a sobering influence in the presence of his gun that makes the armed citizen steer clear of those potentially lethal conflicts which can be avoided by a moral, law-abiding man.

Those of us who have seen violent death up close, who have seen what high-powered bullets can do to living human tissue, have a horror of inflicting that nightmarish, never forgotten damage on a fellow being. Perhaps the only more terrifying prospect is that such a fate should befall us or our loved ones. This is why we, a representative cross-section of America's population, keep deadly weapons for personal defense.

The laws that govern the use of that deadly force in our society are not uniform. They are sometimes frighteningly narrow-minded, sometimes dangerously broad. The only real control exists, not in the lawbooks, but in the individual conscience of the citizen who chooses to arm himself against the grave and present danger of personal, criminal assault.

I can only remember the words of my father on the day I turned twenty-one and applied for my first pistol permit. On that occasion, he presented me with a Smith & Wesson .38 snubnose, and a piece of advice that would guide my own approach to armed defense.

"I hope to Christ you never need to use it," he told me. "But if you ever do—don't miss!"

SUGGESTED READING

In The Gravest Extreme
by Massad F. Ayoob $11.95

Stressfire
by Massad F. Ayoob $11.95

The Semiautomatic Pistol in Police Service and Self-Defense
by Massad F. Ayoob $11.95

Fundamentals of Modern Police Impact Weapons
by Massad F. Ayoob
hardcover $15.95

Hit The White Part
by Massad F. Ayoob $11.95

Gunproof Your Children/Handgun Primer
by Massad F. Ayoob $4.95

The Truth About Self Protection
by Massad F. Ayoob $7.99

Advanced Combat Shotgun: The Stressfire Concept
by Massad F. Ayoob $11.95

Ayoob Files: The Book
by Massad F. Ayoob $14.95

The Street Smart Gun Book
by John Farnam $11.95

Mastertips
by Jon Winokur $11.95

Police Handgun Manual
by Bill Clede $15.95

Police Shotgun Manual
by Bill Clede $15.95

Police Nonlethal Force Manual
by Bill Clede $15.95

Police Officer's Guide
by Bill Clede $19.95

Mostly Huntin'
by Bill Jordan $21.95

No Second Place Winner
by Bill Jordan $14.95

No Second Place Winner
by Bill Jordan
Spanish Edition $15.95

Armed And Female
by Paxton Quigley $5.99

Prices and availability subject to change without notice.

To order or to obtain a more updated version of our catalog, please write to POLICE BOOKSHELF, P.O. BOX 122, CONCORD, N.H. 03302-0122 or call our toll free 1-800-624-9049. In state, call 603-224-6814. We accept MasterCard, Visa, American Express, or Discover credit cards. Please add $4.90 to cover shipping and handling costs.